When Values Conflict

Essays on Environmental Analysis, Discourse, and Decision

Published for the American Academy of Arts and Sciences
a companion volume to *When Values Conflict*
Feiverson, H.A., F.W. Sinden, R.H. Socolow eds.
Boundaries of Analysis: An Inquiry Into the Tocks Island Dam Controversy

When
Values
Conflict

Essays on Environmental
Analysis, Discourse, and Decision

Edited by:
Laurence H. Tribe
Corinne S. Schelling
John Voss

Published for the American Academy of Arts and Sciences

Ballinger Publishing Company • Cambridge, Mass.
A Subsidiary of J.B. Lippincott Company

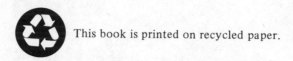 This book is printed on recycled paper.

"This book was prepared with the support of National Science Foundation Grant No. ESR 72-03540. However, any opinions, findings, conclusions or recommendations expressed herein are those of the authors and do not necessarily reflect the views of NSF."

International Standard Book Number: 0-88410-431-1

Library of Congress Catalog Card Number: 75-45448

Printed in the United States of America

When Values Conflict.
    Bibliography: p.
    Includes index.
    1. Environmental policy—United States—Addresses, essays, lectures.
    2. Social values—Addresses, essays, lectures.
HC110.E5W5   333.7   75-45448
ISBN 0-88410-431-1

❈ Contents

✳ Acknowledgments

This book and the companion volume, *Boundaries of Analysis: An Inquiry into the Tocks Island Dam Controversy*, are the products of a several-year study which the American Academy of Arts and Sciences was able to carry out in part because of a grant from the National Science Foundation, under its Research Applied to National Needs (RANN) program. On behalf of the Academy, we want in particular to express our gratitude to Dr. Larry W. Tombaugh, Division of Advanced Environmental Research and Technology, NSF, whose broad experience in environmental problems, continuing interest in our project, and perceptive criticisms of our efforts as they developed were major factors in shaping this study.

We want also to express appreciation to the many people who participated at one stage or another in the series of meetings at which the ideas for the essays in this volume and the companion volume germinated and gradually took shape. Although we cannot mention all of them here, we must make an exception in the case of several who were particularly helpful to the editors and authors. Special acknowledgment is due to Bruce Ackerman, Raymond Bauer, Alvin Enthoven, Leo Marx, Guy Pauker, Wallace Stegner, Lynn White, Jr., and Richard Zeckhauser, each of whom in his own way made a unique contribution to the contents of this and the companion volume. And, as all of those involved in this study know, it was Murray Gell-Mann of the California Institute of Technology who started us on our way by asking some very difficult questions. Finally, had it not been for the generosity of the Committees on Research Funds of the American Academy we could not have accepted the challenge that Professor Gell-Mann's questions posed and undertaken the essential exploratory stages of this project to the point where a coherent study plan emerged.

The Editors

❋ Preface

This collection of essays is an outgrowth of discussions that began nearly five years ago. Although the formal process in which those discussions were embedded terminates with the publication of this volume, concern over the issues raised seems unlikely to end in the near future. Neither a reflection of consensus nor even a representation of the individual authors' final views, the essays collected here can be understood only as interim statements of the conclusions each author has reached thus far with respect to an elusive and enormously complex set of questions.

To define those questions properly is itself no mean task; if this preface begins obliquely, it does so precisely because the questions addressed by the volume it introduces are not easily formulated— perhaps the only conclusions to which every author represented here could subscribe without reservation.

Our inquiry began in late 1970 with an initial question posed by Murray Gell-Mann of the California Institute of Technology: If, as then seemed likely, a new national environmental research institute were to be established to provide analysis and guidance for policy makers, how should it go about its work? By what methods, with what institutional arrangements, and with what kinds of intellectual resources might such an institute hope to perform its analyses with adequate sensitivity to "fragile" values, such as those of preserving wilderness and endangered species? How might such an institute then hope to influence public decision making in directions consistent with such sensitivity? Professor Gell-Mann asked the American Academy of Arts and Sciences to sponsor several exploratory meetings to address these questions. The group organized by the Academy included individuals from many intellectual traditions, representing a range of disciplines from the natural and social sciences to the humanities, each of which we felt might contribute special insights into a complex problem.

What united the members of this initial planning group was not simply a fascination with Gell-Mann's question and a sense of its importance in dealing with a rapidly growing number of disputes at the local, regional, and national level involving the environment; there was also the recognition that the difficulty of dealing with "fragile" values was critical for analysis and decision making in many other areas of national policy, areas as diverse as highway safety and medical ethics.

Quite early in our conversations, we came to realize that the problem under discussion was at once conceptual and institutional: the analytic techniques on which an environmental institute could draw—like the legal, bureaucratic and political frameworks into which its advice would have to fit — were likely to be biased against the adequate representation of some sorts of interests, values, or concerns, and in favor of others. Thus "hard" values, such as short-term economic efficiency, would be likely to swamp "soft" values, such as ecological balance, and even "softer" ones, such as the love of natural beauty. Regretting that prospect, we tried both to understand its causes and to project possible remedies—to discover ways of doing, and of effectively implementing, what Gell-Mann provocatively described as "systems analysis with heart."

As our sessions progressed, and as we exchanged memoranda on the themes defined by our first discussions, our sense of the problem itself underwent a subtle transformation. Some of us at first (and later all of us) began to wonder just what *were* the "fragile" values that we feared technological and economic analysis and political bargaining would dwarf. What, for example, was the common factor among the following interests that made the values they represented difficult to incorporate into traditional modes of analysis and political decision: the preservation of a dying species of whale, the love of wilderness and natural beauty in the northern Cascades, the desire for privacy and retreat in the Maine woods, the maintenance of ecological balance in the Everglades, the energy needs of future generations, even the call of national pride in a monumental engineering venture like the SST? Were such concerns being properly addressed by techniques originally designed to evaluate water quality, employment and recreation needs, or the need for mass transportation? Were professionals originally trained to consider such issues capable of dealing adequately with different ones? Were these interests given adequate weight in the decision-making process? And how was "adequate weight" to be determined?

Furthermore, we asked (and still cannot answer, as the essays in this volume indicate) how are these values best described: as human? fragile? abstract? unquantifiable? environmental? humane? soft? If saving whales and preserving wilderness represent "soft" concerns, in what sense are flood control, or "helping ghetto dwellers," any "harder"? And might not hardheaded economic analyses show the foolhardiness of at least some projects that were ecologically unsound, while richer and more "humane" analyses might make some of these projects seem worthwhile on other than economic grounds?

We began to see that the central question we needed to address was how to resolve value conflicts as such. The issues involved in certain conflicts—for example, those between what are generally accepted to be "hard" and "soft" values (between, say, industrial development and preserving natural beauty)—were in some ways easy to articulate if not to resolve. But environmental disputes also involve conflict among what might be considered competing "soft" values, such as the value of preserving wilderness trails as against the liberty and autonomy of trail-bikers or even hikers seeking refuge from bureaucratic regulation. Gradually we arrived at a somewhat altered vision of the issue before us. We no longer believed, for reasons outlined in some of the following essays, that values or goals could usefully be separated into the "fragile" and the "hardy" such that those associated with one were superior but were harder than the other to "incorporate" into analysis and decision making.

We were thus prepared by our third or fourth meeting to redefine the question at hand. What emerged was a sense that the problem we had been grappling with involved *not* a particular subset of endangered and noble values but rather the realm of values as a whole. It was not so much that the analytic and legal tools available to us inherently skewed policy choices toward some kinds of values and away from others (though some of us continued to find that a troubling possibility); it was that those tools, however well designed for the relatively technical task of finding suitable measures for achieving agreed-upon ends, seemed inadequate to the task of explicitly addressing controverted issues of value *at all*. Indeed, they were not designed to deal with such conflicts.

A cost-benefit analysis, for example, of a proposal for a dam or an oil refinery is simply not a means of resolving a true conflict between competing values. An analysis that purports to calculate the net "benefit" or "cost" of the project as a whole—its overall score on the systems analyst's "objective function"—*assumes* that there is a general agreement on values, at least on the basic values in terms of which costs and benefits to various affected groups are defined and measured, and also on the values that determine how the affected interests are to be compared and weighed against one another. However useful a tool of analysis might be as a means of enabling each affected party to perceive and articulate where its own best interests lie with respect to a problem or proposal, the utility of such a tool as a method of selecting a specific solution for all parties to agree upon or at least to accept is always dependent on a basic agreement among value perspectives.

Inherited from an era when certain basic values and ideals seemed to be more clearly (if tacitly) understood and widely (if not universally) shared, the intellectual and institutional techniques available to the proposed institute of environmental studies—or indeed to *any* policy-oriented research institute—seemed distinctly ill adapted to the task of helping to reach important decisions in a more fragmented society, a society which, for a variety of reasons, was no longer confident about the priorities among its values, and which was becoming increasingly aware of the inherent difficulty of choosing among values in conflict, coupled with the increasingly unavoidable need to do so. Thus with regard to environmental disputes, value conflicts may have been submerged in the past because of a nearly universal agreement that economic growth and efficiency were desirable ends in themselves, or at least that they were important in whatever system of ends might be pursued. In today's much more fluid situation, competing values, recognized by many as equally valid, are receiving widespread support. The result is an inherent tension and moral ambiguity in any claim about values—a classic instance of Hegel's conflict of right against right.

The issue before the study group formally organized by the Academy thus became one of understanding how analytic and institutional devices might be reshaped to address more directly the kinds of value uncertainties and conflicts that our society in the past—surer of its purposes, less uncertain about the adequacy of available resources and about its own long-range prospects, and with fewer articulate interest groups—could more comfortably ignore. The analyst in these circumstances, we agreed, can rarely if ever remain quite the "neutral" scientist who eschews all value judgement; he will often be required to take a forceful role in articulating values, particularly those that seem hidden or obscure, explaining their implications and suggesting alternative and imaginative solutions to the problems in which they figure. He must ask provocative "what if" questions. In sum, we agreed that specific recognition of the role of values, and of the implications of value conflicts throughout the entire analytic and decision process, would increase the probability that a society in transition could be thoughtful about its goals, most of which are not clearly perceived and may be shrouded in controversy, and thus could retain some measure of intelligent control over the directions in which it was moving.

In order to test against reality our emerging hypotheses about analysis and values, to identify a source of still further hypotheses, and to find a setting in which our conclusions might actually have significant consequences, we resolved to expand our mode of inquiry to include the assessment of a "live" environmental dispute. The controversy over the Tocks Island Dam, which was still very much alive at the time of this writing after over a decade of dispute and delay, provided an ideal subject. A group based at Princeton University began a study of the history of this controversy and of the role that values played in its evolution—a study that has richly complemented the more theoretical work whose tentative conclusions are reported here.

During the life of this Academy study, the two groups worked closely together. The students of the Tocks controversy have provided the authors of this volume with a common basis of data from a case displaying most of the value systems, analytic problems, and bureaucratic processes we have considered. The authors in this volume have contributed conceptual and methodological insights that guided and supported the lines of inquiry in the case study, and, in turn, have been stimulated by the ideas the case study has generated. Thus, although the two volumes stand separately, the development of each was continually dependent on that of the other, an interrelationship reenforced by the fact that Robert Socolow of the Princeton group has chapters in both, while Irene Thomson narrates the Tocks story in this book.

Many of the conclusions of both groups focus explicitly on the breakdown of discourse that we eventually came to identify as one of the central issues before us. Our ways of evaluating policy options, and our ways of implementing policy choices, cannot rise above our ways of *talking* about what is at stake and what is to be done. As bearer of a language and mode of analysis long used to address questions less beset by an evident conflict and indeterminacy among values, our society does not come easily to frank and illuminating interchange about the questions of values that now seem to divide it. Thus it is fitting that the first of the essays to follow these introductory remarks, that by Robert Socolow, is concerned with "failures of discourse," a topic that in some respects embraces all that this volume is about.

But our collective discussions, and our individual research, have pushed many of us further—further along and further apart as well. For however we might agree at the general level represented by Robert Socolow's essay, we begin to disagree once the direction of a more successful "value discourse" is to be specified. For some of us, there can be no satisfactory way of talking about, much less acting upon, issues dominated by value controversy without a commitment, necessarily subjective, tentative, and self-correcting, to an evolving moral conception of man and his relationship to nature. For others among us, the very idea of any such commitment, however evolutionary, seems impractical and abstract; they approach the issues in very different terms. For them, the path of wisdom seems rather to be composed of the incremental and pragmatic steps of improving analytic and decision-making techniques in a direction that, among other things, gives greater recognition to value conflicts and to the possible alternatives that might help resolve them.

Most of us, whatever our more distant aspirations, can find little of immediate operational significance in the relatively abstract "option" of developing a systematic communitywide commitment. We cannot, after all, postpone decisions on environmental disputes—or, indeed, on any of the many other problems where values are in conflict—until we have resolved the deepest philosophical issues they pose, issues that have commanded man's attention for centuries. Thus we all rest most of our hopes for improvement in the short run on a more creative deployment of existing scientific and analytic resources, resources that can often circumvent value conflict and value uncertainty by fashioning options, and perhaps even reshaping preferences, so as to satisfy seemingly irreconcilable constraints.

A host of unanswered questions have surfaced—questions about "nature," its cultural and historic meanings and man's relationship to it; about the place of knowledge and analysis in situations of value conflict; about the actual making of hard choices; and about the evolution of decision processes. We now see the surfacing of such questions as the most vital residue of our work. And all of us see a major role for institutional invention—a topic hinted at but barely developed in the essays that follow—in realizing our varying images of the future. But to deny that those images do indeed vary (convenient as such a denial might be from the perspective of editors straining to find unity and cohesion in a collection of essays) would be to falsify the deepest insights this long and often surprising journey has generated for us all.

The several essays that follow seek to distill those insights in a manner faithful to their tentative and sometimes conflicting character. Necessarily, therefore, the aim must be to stimulate further reflection and research rather than to lay any issue to rest. If these essays achieve that goal even moderately well, they will have more than justified the efforts that they and their many discarded predecessors represent.

LAURENCE H. TRIBE
CORINNE S. SCHELLING
JOHN VOSS

When
Values
Conflict

Essays on
Environmental Analysis,
Discourse, and Decision

✳ Chapter One

Failures of Discourse: Obstacles to the Integration of Environmental Values into Natural Resource Policy*

A Reading of the Controversy Surrounding the Proposed Tocks Island Dam on the Delaware River

Robert H. Socolow

I. ANALYSES ARE NOT ABOUT WHAT PEOPLE CARE ABOUT

Major environmental decisions have a way of getting stuck and staying stuck. The discussions about whether to undertake substantial transformations of natural areas—to bring about new power plants, dams, airports, pipelines, deep water ports—have several pathologies in common. A cluster of detailed technical analyses accompanies the formulation of the program and its initial rush onto the stage; the proponents of the project imply, and generally believe, that all one could reasonably have expected has been done, both to justify the program and to anticipate its pitfalls. As after a carefully planned transplant, the reaction of rejection is slow in coming but grows relentlessly. The analyses are shown to be incomplete, and new analyses starting from different premises are eventually produced by those who wish to stop the program. But, contrary to what one might naively expect, the existence of disparate analyses does not help appreciably to resolve the debate. Rarely are the antagonists proud of their analyses; more rarely still are they moved

*This essay also appears in the companion volume, *Boundaries of Analysis: An Inquiry into the Tocks Island Dam Controversy*, edited by Harold A. Feiveson, Frank W. Sinden, and Robert H. Socolow (Cambridge, Mass.: Ballinger, 1976). The occasional references here to the other essays in that volume do not begin to measure the size of the debt this essay owes to the insights and counsel of my associates at Princeton in that long adventure.

by the analyses of their opponents. The combatants on both sides have been constrained by mandated rules of procedure as well as by the tactics of compromise. Understandably, the politicians in a position to determine the outcome conclude that their time is not well spent pondering the available analyses, even though they may commission still more of them.

The failure of technical studies to assist in the resolution of environmental controversies is part of a larger pattern of failures of discourse in problems that put major societal values at stake. Discussions of goals, of visions of the future, are enormously inhibited. Privately, goals will be talked about readily, as one discovers in even the most casual encounter with any of the participants. But the public debate is cloaked in a formality that excludes a large part of what people most care about.

Analyses are part of the formal debate. We should not be surprised to learn, therefore, that the disciplined analyses brought to bear on a current societal dispute hardly ever do justice to the values at stake. Terribly little is asked of analysis, and analysts respond in a way that allows the potentialities of their disciplines to be undervalued. A recurrent theme in this and the companion volume is that disciplined analysis has enormous unused capability. My sense is that we need to look much more carefully at the reasons why this capability lies unused. There is a dynamic interaction between the demands made and the tools developed. It is not realistic to expect much refinement in tools to occur in the absence of a contemporaneous evolution in the rules of public discourse.

The land use debate I have most pondered, and the source of most of my generalizations, is the debate over whether to build a major rock-fill dam on the Delaware River at Tocks Island, thereby creating a 37-mile-long lake along the New Jersey-Pennsylvania border. The dam was proposed by the Corps of Engineers and was authorized by Congress in 1962. Although land has been acquired, and the National Park Service has arrived on the scene to administer the Delaware Water Gap National Recreation Area that is intended to surround the lake, construction has not yet begun. It may never begin. The likelihood of construction has diminished considerably during the period of our study (roughly 1972 to 1975). However, there is a well-known asymmetry: One can decide over and over not to build a dam; one only need decide *once* to begin construction, and there it is.

I happen to hope that the dam will not be built. Building the dam, it seems to me, would buttress an attitude of impudence toward our natural resources. Not building the dam, on the other hand, would stimulate the development of alternate technologies, intrinsically more respectful of nature, which are ever more urgently needed. Of all the arguments for and against the dam, this need to stimulate a reorientation of our technology is for me the single most compelling one. This essay, in part, seeks to imagine what a technology responsive to an environmental ethic would look like. The search for such a technology is one of the absent features of current analysis.

Laurence Tribe's essay in this volume is replete with insights into why an attitude of impudence toward natural resources pervades our culture quite generally at this time. His essay launches a parallel, and even more neglected, area of investigation—into how our attitudes are affected by going along with plans for a dam's construction or resisting such plans, by choosing to build or choosing not to build.

Others, who hope that the dam *will* be built, are persuaded by arguments with which current analysis is also unconcerned. There are some who sustain a vivid image of the havoc wrought by floods. They regard the rest of us as their wards, who need to be protected from our faulty memories. They are almost surely right in their assertion that if another flood were to strike the Delaware Valley during the remaining period of debate, those in favor of the dam would have a far easier time prevailing. They may be wrong, however, as to whether a program to limit flood damage ought to concentrate its construction on the river's main stem, instead of on its tributaries. I know of no serious analysis that captures the essence of this particular issue.

Others in favor of the dam resonate to the argument Robert Dorfman finds so compelling in his own essay in this volume: the many poor people in the metropolitan areas not very distant from this project have needs deserving priority in federal programs; one of these needs—getting away—is better matched to lake recreation than to river recreation; the preferences of the environmentalists are those of people just a bit too comfortable with themselves and too self-centered. This, too, is a position strongly held, politically salient, and not, to my knowledge, captured by a single piece of sustained analysis. One possible analysis along these lines would explore the institutional, economic, and social factors relevant to a comparison of recreation at Tocks Island Lake with recreation at improved urban facilities, including swimming pools.

There are a wide variety of reasons why those concerned with affecting the outcome of a major land use issue are not envisioning (or at least are not expressing) many of the concerns that in fact move them and many of the options that in fact are open to them. Given the fact that virtually all the participants are dissatisfied with the way discourse currently proceeds, it seems worthwhile to make a substantial effort to understand some of the underlying reasons for these failures of discourse, and some of the possibilities for averting them.

II. BLUNT TOOLS AND SKEWED DISCOURSE

A. Golden Rules

The decision about whether to build Tocks Island Dam is widely perceived to be a choice among alternative conceptions of the region's future and, at a deeper but still articulated level, among alternative conceptions of man's appropriate relationship to nature. The tools that might have assisted in clarifying what the possible futures entail include cost-benefit analysis, which has been designed to facilitate comparisons between programs offering differing streams of future costs and benefits. Working with these tools, as Henry Rowen argues persuasively in this volume, ought to lead to translations of dimly perceived preferences into relatively explicit strategies, and ought to reveal the incompatibility of some sets of aspirations and the compatibility of others. Current practice, however, follows a series of golden rules—prescriptions and routines that the analyst perceives to be a means of simplifying the tangle of options (and of staying out of trouble), but that prevent the analyst from taking full advantage of the capabilities the tools provide.

The best conceivable use of the tools, to be sure, will leave serious problems unsolved. David Bradford and Harold Feiveson, in an essay on cost-benefit analysis in the companion volume, make the useful three-way distinction among "ideal," "best practicable," and "actual" cost-benefit analyses. The abuse of tools through overuse of golden rules creates a gulf between actual and best practicable analyses, to which I return momentarily. But even best practicable cost-benefit analyses are going to have serious shortcomings, which discussions of ideal cost-benefit analysis have often underestimated. Discussions of the limitations of cost-benefit analysis nearly always emphasize uncertainties about the discount rate and contain caveats about the lack of sensitivity regarding who gets what. Only rarely do they call attention to the problem of drawing a boundary around the system being studied. As in idealized thermodynamics, the cost-benefit theory presupposes a system coupled with its surroundings in such a simple way that one can change the system without perceptibly affecting the surroundings. To do a sensible cost-benefit comparison of two alternative futures, one has to include in the "system" all the activities with which are associated large differences depending on which future is being considered.

If one is to compare a future with the Tocks Island Dam to one without it, even the dollar costs are such that one must include the incremental sewage treatment facilities required to coexist with a lake instead of a river, and the extra roads needed to bring the visitors to the recreation area, if lake-based recreation will indeed attract more visitors than river-based recreation. Both these costs, it turns out, are comparable to the cost of building the dam itself (several hundred million dollars). One may also have to include the uncompensated costs endured by the roughly 20,000 residents in the valley whom the reservoir project is displacing. But then what about including, on the other side of the balance sheet, the increases in property values expected if the dam is built? Does the series of new entries terminate, in the sense that one is finally considering effects (such as gross interregional migration?) that, even though large, are still effectively unchanged by the existence or nonexistence of the project? No analysis has convinced me that the series does terminate or converge in this sense.

Golden rules have been developed which shelter the practitioner of cost-benefit analysis from this uncertainty about boundaries. The analysis becomes stylized, like the folk art of an isolated village. Those costs and benefits which it is permissible to include in the analysis become codified, as do many of the procedures for evaluating their dollar magnitudes. The warping effect on discourse is substantial. It is hard not to introduce the project to a newcomer with: "The project has four intended benefits" (water supply, flood control, recreation, and electric power, in this instance).

The formal rules also carry weight in the detailed planning of a project. The Corps of Engineers continues to maintain that the "highest and best" use of the lake requires the provision of recreation facilities on its shores for 9.4 million visitors (actually, visitor-days) per year, in spite of the statement by two successive governors of New Jersey that they will approve the project only if the recreation facilities are scaled down to 40 percent of that figure. The Corps' persistence must be strongly affected by the way the analyses come out when the formal conventions are followed, for recreation comes to almost half the total annual benefits when the higher figure is used. Others in this volume comment on the extraordinary reduction in the problem's structure that occurs when the value of recreation is calculated by multiplying a fixed dollar value per visitor-day ($1.35) with a number of visitor-days per year, irrespective of who the visitors are, or how crowded the facilities are, or whether the same visitor spends several days or several visitors spend one day.[a] Here I wish to emphasize that these oddly formal rules do have real consequences—consequences such as extra roads being built through open country to provide the access needed to keep the park populated.

The rules of procedure that govern the planning process have yet further impact in restricting the search for alternatives. One of the rules, for example, is that, at a given site, either a multipurpose project or a single-purpose project is to be undertaken—and that, once this choice is made, *multipurpose projects are not to be compared with packages of single-purpose projects addressing the same needs.* Invoking this golden rule, the principal government agencies (the Corps of Engineers and the Delaware River Basin Commission) can dismiss a proposal without analysis if it addresses just one of the four intended benefits—even if another, companion proposal addresses the other three. Environmental critics of the Tocks Island Dam have advocated the use of "high-flow skimming" to provide increments to water supply equivalent to those the dam would produce. If one enlarged an existing reservoir (Round Valley) and perhaps built an additional small reservoir in a subsidiary valley, thus filling the reservoirs with Delaware water in high-flow months and emptying them in low-flow months, offstream storage would be achieved and the main stem of the Delaware would remain unblocked.[b] This suggestion, to be sure, does nothing about main-stem flood control, but flood-plain zoning does. The package needs to be placed alongside the Tocks project. Yet high-flow skimming has been dismissed with a single comment: "This is not a multipurpose project."[c]

[a]The dollar values of alternate forms of recreation *are* distinguished; $1.35 is a weighted average of the forms of recreation Tocks will provide.

[b]The proposal was initially suggested by Smith Freeman, a scientist acting as an interested bystander. It was explored in greater detail in a study commissioned by the Environmental Defense Fund, *New Jersey Water Supply: Alternatives to Tocks Island Reservoir* (M. Disko Associates, W. Orange, N.J., October 1973).

[c]The rule operates in another instance that stacks the deck against packages of single-purpose projects. The water supply benefit is quantified as the dollar cost of the least expensive alternative way of providing an equivalent amount of water, and the cost of building this alternative is calculated using a higher discount rate than the discount rate for the multipurpose project. The grounds for using two different discount rates are that the Corps may not build the single purpose project it is evaluating, and any other builder would have to borrow money at a higher rate of interest. (The rates used are 3-1/8% for Corps projects and 4-1/2% for alternative projects.)

When the routine procedures of a government agency are consistent with the perfunctory rejection of ideas emerging from outside its bureaucracy, "noise" is thereby built into the discourse between that agency and its critics. The environmentalist critics have pushed the idea of high-flow skimming harder (and with more success, perhaps, than the idea deserves), because of the inability of the government agencies involved to look at it squarely.

B. Golden Numbers

Environmental discourse likewise manifests a powerful dependence on numbers. A number that may once have been an effusion of a tentative model evolves into an immutable constraint. Apparently, the need to have precision in the rules of the game is so desperate that administrators seize on numbers (in fact, get legislators to write them into laws) and then carefully forget where they came from. Then *no one* wants to reopen an argument that hinges on one of these golden numbers.

In the Tocks case, one such golden number is 3,000 cubic feet per second (cfs), the target minimum flow for the Delaware as it passes Trenton, New Jersey. During the drought years from 1963 to 1965, the flow at Trenton fell below that value for months. (The minimum recorded daily low flow was 1,240 cfs in July 1965.) This happened largely because New York did not live up to an agreement with New Jersey and Pennsylvania, negotiated by a river master appointed by the Supreme Court,[d] to release water from its own reservoirs on the Delaware tributaries so as to sustain a flow of 1,525 cfs (another golden number) at Montague, New Jersey, a little over 100 miles upstream from Trenton. (Not surprisingly, nearby New York City—half of whose water comes from these reservoirs—had grounds to fear a water shortage in the same months.) The salt concentration in the river near Philadelphia increased as a result of this low flow. The Public Health Service standard for drinking water is 250 parts chloride per million parts of water (still another golden number). During the autumn of 1964, the line in the river where this concentration is found crept to within ten miles of the place (called the Torresdale intake) where Philadelphia takes its water supply out of the Delaware.[e]

[d]Amended Decree of the Supreme Court of the United States Re Delaware River Diversion, 347 U.S. 995 (1954). The 1960s drought exceeded the drought of record (in the 1930s) on the basis of which the original agreements had been quantified.

[e]The Torresdale intake is at mile 110.53, and the mean daily 250 parts per million chloride line was found at approximately mile 101 on Nov. 20, 1964,

Somewhere (no one appears to remember the details) it was decided that "3,000 cfs at Trenton" would give everyone a proper margin of safety. And proposed reservoirs upstream from Trenton are now judged in significant part by their ability to provide enough "low-flow augmentation" to assure that 3,000 cfs at Trenton could be achieved if there were another drought like 1963–66. Without the Tocks Island Dam, under a contemporary rerun of the historic drought (but assuming that New York maintains its obligations and that reservoirs built since the drought are utilized), flows at Trenton that stay above 2,700 cfs could be achieved. But the missing 300 cfs, or 10 percent, causes genuine alarm. Even *one* percent values have policy content. Electric utilities are told to provide offstream storage of cooling water for their planned riverfront power plants, on the basis that the associated evaporative losses from cooling (about 30 cfs for a typical 1,000 megawatt electric generating plant with a cooling tower) threaten the 3,000 cfs guideline. A few government officials and utility executives wonder aloud where the "3,000 cfs" number came from, and what they are hoping for is the instatement of some lower number that experts will say is safe for Philadelphia (and for the wells of Camden, New Jersey, across the river).

But to hallow *any* minimum flow is to skew the discourse. Whenever a ground rule of discussion is that some standard or guideline is to be accepted as an on-off number, above which there is "safety" and below which there is "peril," two vital kinds of discourse become illegitimate: discussions of acceptable damage, and discussions of damage limitation.

C. Acceptable Damage

The apparent thrust of engineering is to protect man and his works from nature's assaults. Bridges are to survive the highest winds, buildings are to stay warm on the coldest days. Dams, especially, are perceived as symbols of security, as protectors from both floods and droughts. "When water is stored behind a dam, it is there when you need it, like money in the bank," an old-timer told me. A dam's aura of invincibility derives, no doubt, from its sheer bulk, its monumentality. Yet the image is a most incomplete one, for the reservoir,

---

according to Plate III-1 of *Water Resources Study for Power Systems: Delaware River Basin* (consultants' report prepared by Tippetts-Abbett-McCarthy-Stratton, March 1972). The salinity level falls rapidly with distance in that range of concentrations; it was only 40 ppm at Torresdale on that same (worst) day. The same chloride line at high water slack may have been a mile closer.

which comes along with every dam, is the exemplar of compromise. How high should the reservoir be filled? Too high and a surprise flood will not be contained, too low and the reserve supply will be absent in a drought. From which of the multiple outlets, at varying heights, should water be withdrawn in late summer (when the reservoir is thermally stratified and the deep, cold water is laden with decaying organic matter)? One answer emerges if the goal is to "enhance" the fish life downstream, another if the goal is to remove nutrients that contribute to the eutrophication of the lake; the two goals are unlikely to be perfectly compatible. The hallmark of engineering is the trade-off and the artful compromise.

But people prefer appearance to reality. There is rarely any clamor to make trade-offs explicit; it is enough for many that the compromises reached reflect professional judgment. Public discourse is thus dominated by solutions offered as risk-free. Among his colleagues, an administrator for the Federal Aviation Administration responsible for equipping private airports with traffic control equipment can admit to having a target figure in his head for "acceptable annual fatalities from general aviation operations." And military officers get used to thinking in terms of acceptable losses of troops and materiel. But neither the mayor whose town abuts the airport nor the President preparing the battle plan can use such language with his constituency. The larger the issue of public accountability (as opposed to professional accountability alone) looms in an official's mind, the less willing he becomes even to formulate a problem in terms of acceptable risk. These reflexes persist even when no lives are at stake: thus the desire to find a safe minimum flow so as not to think about tolerable levels of discomfort and dislocation.

Yet the usefulness of phrasing problems in terms of acceptable risk is probably nowhere so obvious as in problems that involve fitting man's activities onto a highly variable natural background. This has been recognized explicitly in some of the air pollution legislation, where standards are typically written in the form: the concentration of pollutant X shall not exceed C_o more than N times each year. The most compelling reason for drawing up probabilistic standards of this sort is to recognize and bend with the variability of atmospheric phenomena; atmospheric inversions, for example, will occur occasionally, with little notice, and will produce a buildup of pollution levels. It may be unreasonable to have so much pollution control equipment in place that on the occasion of the worst inversion on record, the pollution concentration C_o is not exceeded. Put another way, it may be possible to win community acceptance of a C_O that is lower as long as an occasional escape is permitted. Mathematically, having C_O and N to play with instead of just C_O (with N set equal to zero) gives the legislator and the community more options in terms of environmental planning.

The regulation of water use seems not to have manifested the same subtlety of design. Pollution targets are almost invariably set at specific values, rarely even adjusted for the time of the year.[f] Minimum river flows, as specified in rules and procedures without built-in escapes, determine the operation of reservoirs. New reservoirs are judged primarily in terms of their "safe yield." All these simplifications channel the imagination in similar ways. The safe yield of a reservoir is that rate of extraction of water from the reservoir which, under a recurrence of the most severe drought of record, could be sustained continuously. Usually the reservoir, at the extremum of the drought, lies nearly empty.[g] Attention is thus diverted from any consideration of riding with the punch, organizing one's affairs differently when the drought arrives, and leaving the reservoir with most of its water in it.[h]

From the standpoint of public health, there would seem to be no explanation for this distinction between air and water standards. The adverse health effects of air and water pollution are structurally similar: both involve no clear-cut level at which acute reactions ensue, no physiological warning that levels have become toxic, enormous variability among individuals (including certain groups that are especially susceptible), and uncertain synergisms. River flow is an even better example of stochastic (random) variability in nature than are the movements of cold and warm fronts of air. It is perplexing that environmental design reflecting this variability has not arisen. Perhaps the older traditions of water law and the concomitant

---

[f]For a detailed discussion of the remarkable oversimplification of the structure of the pollution problem in the planning for the cleanup of the Delaware estuary, see Bruce Ackerman, Susan Rose Ackerman, James W. Sawyer, Jr., and Dale W. Henderson, *The Uncertain Search for Environmental Quality* (New York: Free Press, 1974).

[g]If a reservoir is constrained by rules of operation to retain some minimum water level, this is incorporated into the calculation of its yield.

[h]The dissonance between the recreation and water supply objectives of the Tocks reservoir has figured prominently in its political history. In those years when "drawdown" of the reservoir would be necessary, mudflats would be exposed at its periphery and the opportunities for recreation correspondingly impaired. The Council on Environmental Quality has called particular attention to this problem, and to the problem of eutrophication (see section III A), in its reviews of the project.

self-images of the "water professionals" are historically inhibiting factors.

The water professionals make continual use of the stochastic concept of the N-year storm, or flood, or drought—one whose severity should be exceeded, on the average, just once in N years. The concept is most often used in situations where N is large (50 or 100 or more) and a decision is to be made about how high to build a levee or how strong to make a mooring buoy. The concept unfortunately happens to be on least secure scientific footing when N is large, because of the shortness and uncertainty of the available hydrological record and the significance of unaccountable changes in topography. The concept is rarely used when N is small, say 10. It would be worth searching for a way of activating an interest in procedures where, say, one year in every ten (with the dates determined by nature), the planned interactions of man with river will be qualitatively different. If the river is ordinarily used for waste removal and for commercial fishing, for evaporative cooling and for drinking water, then during the summer and autumn months of a once-in-ten year of unusual low flow, either the wastes will be removed in a different way (or will be more highly treated or stored) or the commercial fishing will be suspended; and either the power production upstream will be cut back (or another form of cooling used) or the drinking water will be taken from somewhere else.

If one is willing to confront the costs of occasional disruption, one is led quite naturally to modify the usual analyses of the optimal timing of construction of water supply projects. When a positive discount rate is used to relate intertemporal preferences, the result, necessarily, is that it pays to delay any project somewhat beyond the time when it would be needed under the (usual) assumption that the historic worst drought will certainly befall the region the very year that the project is completed.[i]

Once acceptable damage becomes a legitimate subject for discourse, much of the fabric of water resource planning must be rewoven. Projects are deferred with a nonzero probability of their arriving too late; reservoir management proceeds under the expecta-

---

[i]These ideas have been worked out quantitatively, with a highly simplified model of the variable hydrology, in a significant but unpublished Appendix to the Northeastern United States Water Supply Study of the Corps of Engineers, *Economic Analysis for Organization, Legal, and Public Finance Aspects of Regional Water Supply*, 1972. The appendix was prepared by the Institute of Public Administration, New York, N.Y., and, in particular, I believe, by Dr. Ruth Mack.

tion that in low rainfall periods there will be some compromise between drawdown and curtailment of consumption; and consumption is scanned for its lower and higher priority components. The cumulative effect of such a reweaving will be to weaken the insulation of society from natural events. Acceptable damage is disruption of routine at times beyond our choosing: it means brown lawns and fountains empty in droughts, closed highways and downed power lines in floods.

Nature modulating society: is this something we could ever get used to? The thrust of most of industrial society has been in the opposite direction: to reduce man's vulnerability to nature's excesses and, by extension, to reduce man's subordination to nature's variability. The starkest contrast in nature is *dead-alive.* Man has labored hard to be in control of that dichotomy to the largest extent possible; judging from the present concern with the treatment of the terminally ill, man may indeed be overdoing it. But there are lesser contrasts that industrial man has also felt it was his destiny to override, where it is even more certain that we are in sight of a boundary of reasonableness. *Light-dark:* The candle, the electric light, the night shift, the night ball game. *Cold-hot:* Clothing and housing, refrigeration, hothouse fruits and vegetables, air conditioning, heated patios in winter. *Wet-dry:* Boats, dikes, irrigation, umbrellas, humidifiers and dehumidifiers. One could go on—*grass-crabgrass,* overcome by herbicides, *grass-mud,* overcome by artificial turf (and plastic trees!). The shame of a city surprised by an early snowstorm, and of a town faced with a washed-out bridge—might that shame now have become excessive?

The vast majority of us are uncomfortable contemplating even the possibility of deliberately subjecting ourselves to the variability of nature. A representative of the Delaware River Basin Commission finds such a concept "not socially acceptable." Yet, as Charles Frankel and Laurence Tribe make vivid (in two very different ways) in their essays in this volume, the possibility of *success* in insulating ourselves from nature is a horror it is time to confront. Have we indeed instructed the engineers to produce a technology such that no natural event, however rare, would require us to react? Did we really mean to do this?

D. Damage Limitation

When discussion of acceptable damage comes more naturally to the planners, more inventive approaches to *damage limitation* can be expected to follow. In recent years, there has been a start in this direction, promoted in considerable measure by The National

Environmental Policy Act of 1970 (NEPA), which requires the examination of "nonstructural alternatives" to all federally assisted construction programs. The nonstructural alternatives to dams as a means of flood control include· flood-plain zoning, carrot-and-stick flood damage insurance, and early warning systems. At least the first of these has figured prominently in the discourse in the State of New Jersey, whose legislature has passed a flood-plain zoning act as a direct result of a chain of argument originating with the proposal for the Tocks Island Dam.

The nonstructural alternatives to dams as a way of extending water supplies include, above all, strategies to improve water conservation, including metering and charging for water in a way which discriminates between consumptive and nonconsumptive uses and between high and low flow periods. Efforts along these lines have begun recently at the Delaware River Basin Commission. Indeed, part of the water resources community regards the Tocks Island Dam as an old-fashioned project precisely because it fails, by and large, to incorporate the currently more fashionable nonstructural approach to the historic objectives of water management.

But damage limitation strategies are by no means limited to nonstructural strategies. There are "engineering strategies" to minimize the damage of droughts and floods, which nonetheless may involve hardware in the cities instead of hardware in the wilderness. The new state buildings in downtown Trenton in the flood plain of the Delaware were built with their heating and cooling plants on higher floors so that flooding could be withstood. One damage limitation strategy for drought periods for Philadelphia might be to run a pipe upstream ten or even twenty miles, so that water could be taken from the Delaware in a region of lower salinity in the event of a severe drought; in normal times, the pipe would just lie there.[j] Another damage limitation strategy—one that would take much longer to implement and that might apply only to a new or rebuilt city—would be to maintain two parallel water systems, one for uses that require high quality water (drinking, cooking, bathing) and one for uses that can tolerate water of lower quality (many industrial uses, toilet flushing). In so doing, a city would substantially reduce the task of producing enough high quality water.[k] All these are

---

[j]The earliest reference I know that presents this idea is the *Report on the Utilization of the Waters of the Delaware River Basin* (Malcolm Pirnie Engineers—Albright and Friel, September 1950).

[k]An analogous approach to the likely energy problems of the next two decades would seek a means to supply priority users of electrical energy

"structural" or "engineering" solutions; conceivably, the system of parallel piping would be even more complex and costly than a system of dams and reservoirs. The difference, however, lies in the location at which the enterprise is carried out: engineering our urban complexes rather than our wilderness areas and landscapes. Those encouraging the search for nonstructural solutions are largely motivated by a desire to be more gentle to the natural environment; they should be reminded that the same end can often be achieved by a geographic transposition of the technological imagination.

If creative technology should one day return to the cities and there display an increased cybernetic emphasis, we will begin to raise our expectations of the machines around us. We will insist that they last longer, be easier to repair, and undergo a more satisfactory metamorphosis at the end of their lives. We will also learn to insist that our machines report to us more faithfully how they are functioning, so that we know when to repair them or replace them. Finally—and perhaps this is more controversial—we will come to insist that our machines allow us to increase our sensual contact with our natural surroundings.

Of all the impacts of the "energy crisis" of the 1973-74 winter, the most lasting, I predict, will be its impact on architecture. The downtown office building of the 1960s already stands as a metaphor for the whole society's desire for enforced independence from the natural setting: temperature, humidity, air exchange, and lighting are all controlled mechanically, independent of season, wind speed, or whether one is on the north or south side of the building. Neither materials nor design change as the location is moved in latitude by thousands of miles. (In physicists' jargon, the building is invariant under ninety-degree rotations, displacements in space, and translations in time.) The notion of air conditioning a sealed office building on a mild day appears grotesque once one becomes aware that upstream from the power lines there are scarce resources whose extraction and conversion are necessarily accompanied by environmental damage. The office building of the near future will have openable windows, fewer lights and more switches, north-facing walls very different from south-facing walls (the latter having awnings or comparable "soleil briser" projections), and east-facing walls different from west-facing walls if either east or west is the direction of the

---

(hospital facilities, refrigerators, elevators) even in situations of substantial brownout or blackout. As a colleague of mine put it, "invest in switching equipment."

prevailing wind. It may also have solar energy collectors and water collectors on the roof and windmills mounted on the vertical edges. Less symmetry, more deliberate hassle, more life.

I could be wrong. The technology of the near future may instead be designed to refine our sensibilities still further in the directions of change of the past several decades: toward personal security, toward isolating ourselves from our machines, and toward being able to do everything everywhere. Cities connected by cars on rails that arrive empty at your home and leave you at work before they pick up another passenger, heavy cars to make the ride smooth. (The Personalized Rapid Transit systems on the drawing boards are usually presumed to operate under such constraints.) Junking consumer products at the first sign of breakdown. Recreation of all kinds available at all places and all times: outdoor iceskating rinks in the Caribbean, heated swimming pools (heated *lakes*?) for winter swimming in the Adirondacks.

It seems more likely to me that we are in the early stages of an intellectual and cultural sea change. Images of saturation of wants go only part of the way toward explaining why the near future should not be predictable by a straightforward extrapolation of the recent past. For part of what is involved is the development of new wants and the rediscovery of ancient ones, a development that Laurence Tribe and Robert Dorfman sketch in their essays as a kind of "groping upward." An important class of new wants that is already palpable expresses a desire for interaction with "the only earth we have." These wants will call into being still uninvented technologies, public policies, and styles of discourse appropriate for such a resource-respectful new world.

III. THE SPECIAL PROBLEMS OF ECOLOGY

Biological information can be relatively easily tracked by the observer of decision making, in part because it is less emotionally charged than political or economic information, so people will talk about it, and in part because it is still novel, so people tend to have clear impressions of what they know and where they've learned it. Accordingly, the study of how biological information is processed in the course of making decisions about the use of natural resources ought to give insight into how other kinds of information are processed as well. In three matters—eutrophication, shad, and oysters—ecology has played a prominent and visible role in decision making.

A.   Eutrophication of Tocks Island Lake

Tocks Island Lake, so named at the time of its conception, may turn out to have poor prospects for a healthy existence. Other reservoirs in the region regularly eutrophy in the late summer—that is, they develop pockets of foul smelling weeds along their shores. Rivers are intrinsically easier to take care of; they train themselves. The key quantitative parameter is the flushing time—the mean residence time for the water (and hence for any nutrients entrained in the water) from time of entry to time of exit. It is measured in *months* for a lake and in *days* for a river.

If the shoreline is coated with scum, the lake's value for recreation will be greatly impaired. This direct connection between biology and people has made the issue of eutrophication the pivot for large political motions. Eutrophication provides the opponents of a dam with the first argument that matches flood control in its capacity to embarrass: signs saying *Highway Flooded* with a dam unbuilt and signs saying *Beach Closed* with a dam built are both distressing images, and the politician instinctively shuns association with either of them. He cares about embarrassment a lot more than about the possible need to recompute the number of recreation visitor-days, but the two are linked.

The eutrophication issue has implicated the upstream bystander, New York State, in a new way. The nutrients carried in the runoff from poultry farms and municipalities far above the dam site would be trapped in the lake, where they could contribute substantially to the stimulation of unwanted biological growth. The votes of New York's politicians, including its governor (a member of the Delaware River Basin Commission) are now cast more cautiously, for the expenses of controlling runoff are considerable. Ecology has shrunk the distances along the river, involving those over 100 miles upstream from the dam in the fate of those beside the dam and (as will be seen below) with the fate of those over 100 miles downstream from the dam as well.

But the reservoir may not eutrophy. Systematic measurements of the mineral content of the inflows into the Delaware and its tributaries are only just beginning, and it is not possible to make even an educated guess. In all the data available in 1973, there were just twenty measurements of phosphorus (the most critical nutrient) in the entire reach of the river where the lake would form. The extraordinary casualness about data acquisition is a significant phenomenon in its own right. It is especially mystifying in a setting where the same people who are casual about data are found commissioning a procession of technical reports on the subject of eutrophication. The earliest of these, the "McCormick Report," carries a lament at the sorry condition of the data and pleads that something be done before the next report is commissioned.[1] Thomas Cahill, two years after participating in the writing of the McCormick Report, found the "resistance by the responsible agencies" to undertaking programs of data acquisition in the field "stubborn, almost irrational."[2] In the past three years, the Corps of Engineers has spent its research funds on an elaborate computer model, *Lakeco*,[3] and on a study of how eutrophication, if it were to occur, could be cleaned up.[4]

With the introduction of *Lakeco*, the discourse about Tocks Island Lake may demonstrate new pathologies. Computer output has a way of paralyzing those who look at it, at least temporarily. The output of *Lakeco* takes the form of graphs of biological load in the lake versus month of the year, for various assumptions about inputs of nutrients; it appears to give the answers the political process needs. To the credit of the Corps and its contractor, *Lakeco* has been published with complete annotation, and the computer deck has been made available to interested bystanders. Nonetheless, there is no institutional mechanism to provide a critique of the report, which is full of patently unjustified assumptions. The model is an exercise, a milestone in a developing art. It has not yet carried more weight in the political process than it deserves, but it stands unchallenged, waiting to be believed.[1]

B. Shad

The shad, like many species of salmon and trout, is anadramous— that is, it spawns in fresh water and lives most of its life at sea. One of its spawning areas is above the site of the dam. The shad problem was recognized from the outset of the project, and has been dealt with in the traditional fashion: a fish ladder was included in the dam project. It was acknowledged that most of the shad trying to use the spawning area would not get there or that their offspring would not get back to the ocean. The ladder, however, was clearly better than nothing and was not very costly. The shad was acknowledged to be abundant elsewhere, to be subject to numerous other hazards (such as those encountered in navigating the stretch of water with low

---

[1]Three of my colleagues on this research project, Robert Cleary, Daniel Goodman, and Douglas Zaeh, have been investigating *Lakeco* and its application to Tocks Island Lake. It is possible that their critique of the model's hydrology and biology (in the companion volume) will check the usual tendency of models of this kind to carry unjustified weight. But such matters obviously should not be left to the chance attentions of a nearby research group.

dissolved-oxygen content in the polluted Delaware estuary), and to be replaceable (at least from the fisherman's standpoint) if a program of stocking the lake behind the dam were undertaken.

To many builders of dams, fish ladders represent "going the extra step" to accommodate their environmentalist critics, and to placate the environmentalist in themselves. At some dams in the west, a visitors' gallery is installed from which the fish can be watched as they climb. Evidently, our fascination with their strength and determination overrides our dismay that we are putting them through such paces. Or perhaps debates ensue in the galleries—I should like to know—and consciousness is raised. To some ecologists, however, fish ladders represent kidding yourself. You see fish climb the ladder successfully, but you do not see them lost in the lake, or (even more likely) their offspring unable to find their way back downstream. Both migrations are keyed to fast-moving water.

How can such incompatible perspectives continue to coexist? Fish ladders appear to provide the means for resolving the conflict, for they usually double as devices for counting fish, keeping score each season. With so many fish-ladder-years of experience behind us, we must have some respectable quantitative information about how various ladders affect the numbers of fish arriving each year, sorted by species, by distance upriver, by month of the year. Or are ecologists unwilling to consider such data respectable? Ecologists are wary of quantitative indices of performance, for they are oriented to a world full of nonlinearities and thresholds. If the population climbing a fish ladder drops annually an average of 5 percent over several seasons, the ecologist will not agree that one could infer the number of years it would take for the population to drop to one-fourth, because a later drop could be abrupt. "No one knows the minimal oceanic population necessary for the survival of the species."[m] The ecologist thus spreads a pall of ominous uncertainty over the entire enterprise of environmental planning. Still, it is curious how little attempt is made to make the argument quantitative.[5]

C. Oysters

The fate of the Delaware Bay oyster is bound up with the dam much as is the shad's. A routine approach analogous to the fish ladder does not exist in this instance, however, and the discourse on oysters has accordingly been more inventive and more bizarre. The oyster beds, 150 miles downstream from the dam, are in a

---

[m]This was Lincoln Brower's response to an early draft of this essay.

deteriorated condition relative to 50 years ago, and they are menaced by a predator known as the oyster drill. It is widely believed that the seasonal high flows of fresh water down the Delaware and into the Bay in April, May, and June are protecting the beds from further assault by the drill, because the oyster is able to tolerate less saline water than the oyster drill and hence gets rid of the drill during that season.

Except for one year in 60, the lake behind the dam is supposed to be full before the spring months of high flow begin. Thus the natural flows (except flood flows, defined as flows in excess of 70,000 cfs) are expected to pass through the dam undiminished each spring. Between the dam and the oysters, however, water is expected to be withdrawn for out-of-basin shipment. The continuity of out-of-basin diversion provided by the reservoir constitutes a major justification for the dam. This diversion can only continue during the spring months at the expense of the water flow to the oysters. Thus, advocates of oysters and advocates of out-of-basin regional growth are potential adversaries.[n]

No one who understands this conflict of interest appears willing to break the news to those who don't. Once, searching vainly for an analysis of this conflict, I was told by a minor Corps functionary, "Who can put a price on the life of a fish?" Yet, within the Corps, it is clear that the overconstrained character of the oyster problem is recognized. With quintessential American optimism, however, the Corps is trying to find a way to *improve* the oyster beds, a way to get them back to their state of 50 years ago, or even better. The Corps is hoping to find a way to do this through a procedure of timed releases of fresh water, all through the year.

The presupposition of such a study is that man can improve on nature. Among conservation groups, however, the oyster issue has had a completely different symbolism. The oyster's dependence on an annual pulse of fresh water is regarded as an *indicator* of the dependence of an entire estuarine ecosystem on that same annual pulse. The life cycles of myriad organisms are tied to these seasonal

[n]By the hydrologist's measure, the Tocks Island Dam, relative to its basin, is not big. To further even out the uneven flow would have required larger storage capacity, and the dam is *not* larger primarily to avoid either drowning or diking Port Jervis, 37 miles upstream. The construction of additional storage capacity on- or offstream should be expected if the goal continues to be to increase the "yield" (the minimum continuously deliverable flow) from the river valley; the yield is maximized only when the flow is completely evened out. Each future storage area will present the same trade-off problem: uneven flow for the oysters, steady withdrawal for man.

fluctuations, and even if another way could be found to protect the oysters from the drill (by chemical or biological control, for example), there would still be other kinds of damage in the estuary if the fresh water pulse were removed. The presupposition here is that man can only diminish the quality of the natural environment by his intervention—that "nature knows best." Although logically inadequate as a guide to problems such as pollution control, in which one intervention of man is designed to reduce the consequences of another, the presupposition is nonetheless a touchstone for a large number of "preservationist" attitudes, which contravene the prevailing interventionist attitudes of most foresters, fisheries managers, and other environmental scientists.

So, whither has policy evolved in this new Age of Ecology? The Corps of Engineers now explores the ecological consequences of its projects. The Fish and Wildlife Service of the U.S. Government intervenes on man's behalf whenever either commercial fishing (oysters) or sports fishing (shad) is threatened. The Corps, in response, reformulates the task of protecting a fishing resource into the task of enhancing it. The Corps consults with leading biologists. It is a new Corps, a more and differently responsive bureaucracy, and, far more than previously, there is a biological dimension to decision making.

The economists tear their hair. What happened to costs and benefits and to the market—to transfer payments to the oystermen, for example, if their beds are destroyed, or payments *by* the oystermen if the beds are improved? There is nothing intangible or fragile about oystermen, so why should traditional methods of economic analysis suddenly be abandoned?°

The conservationists tear *their* hair. Their starting point is piety and self-doubt in the face of nature, and somehow it has gotten lost. To gain entry into the discourse, they talk about a cash crop; to avoid sounding softheaded, they fail to emphasize that, in their view, the "cash crop" is merely an indicator of the condition of a far more valuable ecosystem. The conservationists have separate languages for talking to one another, to politicians, and to their avowed oppo-

---

°To be sure, there are intangible values at stake in the survival of the villages whose local economies are entirely dependent on the oysters, villages with pride, tradition, and people having untransferable skills. Such costs are like the costs of burying under water some of the historic farming villages upstream from Tocks, costs that the present-day cost-benefit analysis appears not to be equipped to incorporate.

nents. Except when they talk to one another (and perhaps even then) they refrain all too often from articulating what really matters to them.

"Professionals," according to one definition, "don't back one another into corners." "I'd rather argue a point of procedure than a point of substance," another professional told me. Self-censorship is a tactic that keeps coalitions together and keeps opponents on speaking terms. But self-censorship, nonetheless, has considerable costs. Some of the costs are political. When a dialogue proceeds under false pretenses, its participants rapidly grow bitter; if after much effort you have scored a point, and your opponent acts as if the score is unchanged (because it really is), you want to quit. The Philadelphia office of the Corps now feels this way about the Environmental Defense Fund, and expresses a strong desire to keep its distance.

At another level, perhaps even more vital, the cost of the conservationist's failure to articulate what most troubles him is the loss of crucial information in the decision process. Many people outside the conservation groups assume that ecological insights are the property of conservationists and are up to them to introduce into the discourse. But what if they don't want to? Once, among conservationists planning strategy, I asked whether floods were beneficial to the life on the river banks. I was told to stop wasting everyone's time; the answer was obviously yes, there was a good movie that showed why,[6] and "this is not what one whispers in the governor's ear." Well, why *not* whisper this into the governor's ear? If the river banks will deteriorate, the governor should know it. If ecologists don't really know, but think they know how to find out, then the support of such research should get high priority.

The question, "Do ecologists really know anything useful?" is on many people's minds. The answer appears to be that, at the very least, they can distinguish among what they know with assurance, what they have hunches about, and what "pop" concepts they see no evidence for whatever. As long as their knowledge is not systematically incorporated into environmental discourse, the United States can continue unfolding its environmental programs and then folding them up again, acting as if only distributive issues and not "real" consequences (duck hunters' votes and not ducks) are at stake. Do estuarine ecosystems become less productive or just different when dams are built? I have the impression that most ecologists believe they know the answer to that one—that indeed a lot *can* be said about how an estuary is damaged when it is simplified; if so, the information may be too important to be left to the conservation groups to introduce.

The ecologists may not have welcome news (indeed, one of the first anthologies on ecology was called *The Subversive Science*), but they must be encouraged to speak, and they must be *questioned*. They have had something essential to say about DDT, and about predator control programs; in the process, we have all learned about food chains. By clarifying the importance of rhythms in nature, ecologists may cause us to rethink some of the practices that have grown up around the assumption that it is invariably to man's advantage to smooth out nature's peaks and valleys. To take a single example, the whole basis of the bartering between interests representing different river basins may be built on faulty ecological principles. The crux of this bartering is the concept that if you take water out of a basin when water is abundant, you must promise to return water to the basin (by releases from a reservoir) when water is scarce. (This is the sort of arrangement New York City has with New Jersey and Pennsylvania, as described in Section II B, above.) The result, if the agreement is respected, is that river flow is evened out. But a river that flows evenly is not a natural river, however convenient it may be to man; plants and animals, in countless well-understood ways, are keyed to the seasonal flow engendered by melting snow. By various yardsticks such as species diversity or production of desired species, the evening of flow could be judged to have deteriorated the river. The repayment with low-flow augmentation could be judged to have negative value.[P]

Ecologists may have something even more disturbing to say about the benefit nature derives from her most *extreme* variations, such as forest fires and floods, as opposed to her regular seasonal variations. If redwoods have depended on periodic forest fires to clear away the understory, and if mangroves have depended on floods to propagate to new locations, what is man to make of such information? The benefits of nature's excesses come as a surprise to those of us who grew up in a culture that emphasized that what was destructive in nature it was man's responsibility to tame (like his temper). The benefits of seasonal flow are less difficult to appreciate; after all, we have our own daily and monthly clocks built in.

[P]A system of values that elevates man's convenience is flawed in other ways, as Charles Frankel reminds us in his essay in this volume: the very enterprise of bringing some of nature's rhythms under deliberate control takes something important from our experience of the world.

IV. IF I LEARN TO LISTEN, YOU MAY
LEARN TO CONVERSE

A. People Are Imagining Futures Very Different
From One Another

- A man high in the Corps of Engineers says, "Either there is a problem with this valley or there isn't one." He means that the valley has many rivers and streams that with little notice can cause destruction and loss of life, more severe with each passing year because of the way land development increases the speed of storm runoff. He also means that the available water supply, if no further dams are built, is going to inhibit regional economic development; perhaps the permanent underground aquifers are already being depleted.
- A Park Service official shows his visitors a sloping cornfield upstream from the dam site and describes how it will become a site of "quality recreation" when the lake fills in: the site will become a beach (it has just the right slope) and, between it and the parking lots, there will be self-guided nature walks, ecology exhibits, shops where local craftsmen will display their works, and the oldest houses and barns of the region, transplanted to these places of highest frequency visitation so that the maximum number of people can become involved. "If the dam isn't built and there isn't a lake here to attract visitors," he argues, "the National Park Service has no business being here."
- A planner in a state agency says, "If we hadn't gotten the federal government into the area, the whole riverfront would have been overwhelmed by land developers, carving up the area for second homes. Until that far-off time when local zoning is effective, we have no choice but to get the federal government involved in restricting the area's development."
- A local mayor tells an inquiring commissioner that he doesn't see how his town can afford another ambulance to handle the accidents that the increased traffic on his roads will generate, and that a majority of his constituents oppose the dam because, with all those city people coming through, each will have to get a lock for his front door.[q]
- A Washington-based planner says, "The number of people who live in New Jersey and commute to work in New York City is too large already. If we don't build the dam, the regional economic and population growth will be slower, and the country will be the better for it. Some of the people who would otherwise have moved to New Jersey from the states in the middle of the country will stay there and some of the people who are leaving New York City will go on past New Jersey

[q]In a referendum in November 1972, in Warren County, New Jersey, which includes the dam site but little of the land that would be flooded. 9,218 people approved the construction of the dam and 14,864 opposed it.

to live in those same states; otherwise, those states will soon be losing population."

• An ecologist worries that managing the water quality in the lake behind the dam will be a continual headache, and that asking for the lake to be suitable for recreation as well as water supply is compounding the problem, both because the visitors' activities add to the waste load entering the lake and because the visitors' activities require higher minimum water quality standards to be met.[r] He also comments, "The river is an organic unit, and now flows well over three hundred miles with hardly an obstruction. Plugging it up at mile 217 will alter the entire structure of interdependence of upstream and downstream life."

• A scoutmaster says, "The valley is perfect just as it is for getting boys and girls from suburbia into the woods for a weekend, where they won't see many people and can learn to take care of themselves. You can't find a better place for beginners to learn canoeing near here either."

• A conservationist says, "We've got to learn to accommodate to nature sometime; why not start here, while there is still some room to maneuver? If the dam is built, nuclear power plants will follow, plants now foreclosed because of the undependable flow in the dry season; that's just pushing your luck. If the dam isn't built, a lot of promising ideas about how we should accommodate to natural limits, like water metering and recycling, flood plain zoning, effluent fees for pollution discharge, energy conservation technologies, and staggered work weeks, will get a more serious hearing. The better ideas will be sorted out from the worse ones while there is still little risk in experimentation." (In the Corps' calculation of recreation benefits, it is assumed that 32 percent of the annual visits to the National Recreation Area will occur on just fourteen days—summer Sundays.)[7]

• An esthete says, "You can see over twenty miles across the valley on a clear day, and there's hardly a work of man in sight. There's no other view of rolling hills anything like the one looking out over Wallpack Bend. And downstream, where each Christmas Washington's crossing is reenacted, you still see the river as it flowed in 1776 (though the bridge right at the spot does detract somewhat); even if only for its place in history, wouldn't the Delaware be a good river to leave unmanaged?"

Out of such conflict, what resolution? It is presumptuous to give blithe answers, but to offer no answers at all is irresponsible. I join several of the other authors in this volume in believing that, as a modest first step, it is worth trying to refine the ways in which the participants in such discourse are assisted by the available technical

---

[r]The Cannonsville Reservoir on the west branch of the Delaware is currently used for water supply and also develops "nuisance blooms of blue-green algae" in the summer. Recreation on the reservoir is not permitted.

information. The basic methods of science, for all but a very few participants, are not themselves controversial. If some consensus can be achieved over matters of geophysics (hydrology in the Tocks case, meteorology in many other land use disputes), matters of biology, and, perhaps, matters of economics, then it is possible that a foundation for productively confronting ever more sensitive layers of the debate could be established. Even by itself, the exercise of ordering the existing disagreements according to a hierarchy of arguability may be salutory.

B. Models and Data Must Be Located in More Helpful Places

A moderate amount of science and an enormous amount of data usually pertain to a given policy decision related to natural resources. In the case of the Tocks Island Dam, historical flows of the Delaware at several gauging stations are available stretching back many decades. The historical record can be restated in stochastic form (giving the probability of recurrence of various degrees of flooding and drought, among other things) and can be "rerun" on a computer with any desired assumption about reservoir releases, out-of-Basin shipments, consumptive losses, and so forth. The water professionals agree with one another to a very large extent concerning how their analytical tools should be used, and the approach they take is not particularly dependent on who the client is: anyone's preferred strategy for management of the river's water flows would be analyzed in essentially the same way. Not only are the data base and the analytical procedures common property resources; so too are the problems of uncertain and missing data, of extrapolation, and of oversimplification in modelling.

One might expect analysts occasionally to be encouraged to assume a neutral stance and to generate an array of results flowing from deliberately varied starting assumptions representative of several conflicting points of view. But this does not in fact happen. One reason, I believe, is that expertise is so widely presumed to be the captive of the adversaries. The model of the court of law is devastating: we have come to expect an insanity trial to produce a psychiatrist for the defense and a psychiatrist for the prosecution. Some environmental expert is presumed to be available who will come out with any answer for which a combatant is willing to pay. The analyst's results are presumed to be little more than the packaging of opinion and sentiment.

Although such attitudes are more often accurate than one might wish, they represent a significant exaggeration. And the costs of such attitudes are high indeed. Not only does a common ground among adversaries fail to be established, but, perhaps just as serious, a constituency for nurturing the data base and the analytic techniques fails to develop. No one in a position to do anything about it cares whether measurements are made or not. Yet almost inevitably, because new issues keep arising, critical data are missing. After years of consultants' reports pleading for the taking of data on the flow of nutrients into the river (as discussed in section III), such a program is still not underway, in spite of the fact (or perhaps because of the fact) that the politically most troublesome technical issue in the current Tocks debate—the likelihood of eutrophication of the reservoir behind the dam—largely depends for its resolution on the availability of such data.

The most unfortunate cost of excessively disparaging the technical tools is the discouragement of sustained efforts to generate alternatives. When a computer stores large blocks of historical flow data and a few elementary routing routines, it cries out to be played with. Questions of the "What If" variety, the seeds of all inventive proposals, are all but certain to germinate if such an invitation is accepted. Yet, today, the ground is not fertile. No one wants to hear. No one has such play as his work.

It is worth looking hard for ways to activate the better use of the relevant "hard science" in policy making. One obvious possibility would be to dissociate the experts from the historic adversaries, in at least a few institutions. Suppose that, in each major river basin, a facility could be established and nurtured which at the least would house the hydrological capability I have just described as well as, presumably, comparable demographic, social, economic, and ecological data banks and software. It is conceivable that, over time and abetted by the staff of such a facility (who would of course seek to justify their existence), the facility would find ways to be useful to a wide range of clients. At such a Center for the Delaware River Basin, the Greater New Jersey Chamber of Commerce, Trout Unlimited, the City of New York, the Environmental Defense Fund, all could come to refine their preferences.

The staff of such a facility would press for further data gathering and model development, and might logically take responsibility for this enterprise. But monitoring the modelers must also be accomplished somehow. There is a market in elaborate computer models today, and it resembles the market in dangerous toys; there is something a little unsavory about sellers and buyers alike.

The seller may have initially developed his model for a research problem to which it was relatively well suited, and the buyer may have begun with a policy problem an appropriate model could clarify. But bargains are struck when there is no match possible. Perhaps the necessary input data do not exist; perhaps the model has structural limitations (inadequate grid size, dimensionality, time dependence); perhaps the positivist character of the output is certain to blind the recipient to its defects. At an earlier time, before computers, it was harder to lose track of a model's uncertainties and imperfections. The water professionals resorted to physical analog models, scaled and distorted, equipped with faucets, wave generators, bottom rougheners, and other hardware. But today's numerical models are often not significantly better in fact at prediction, especially when they are run under a constraint of "modest cost." It is worth thinking about how to structure a center for modeling so that it has incentives to be candid about its models' shortcomings.

The structuring of improved environmental discourse poses other problems of institutional design that can only be touched on here: sources of financial support for the facility, the merits of embedding the facility within a university or national laboratory, its relation to existing facilities, and the confidentiality of both the data and the assistance rendered the clients. The facility should almost surely retain a "service" character, like the Library of Congress, rather than becoming itself the generator of policy. The best (most thorough, most inventive) analysis will usually be demanded only by those who have a stake in the outcome (whether bureaucratic, financial, or emotional), and it would surely be unwise (even if possible) to create a facility that becomes so smart that all the initiative passes to it.

Even those with no initial stake in the outcome can often be helpful: they ask usefully awkward questions. One would like to build in a role for them. I have twice been part of a group of such outsiders, and in each case we left behind us a considerable alteration in perceptions.

In a 1969 summer study run by the National Academy of Sciences, a group of us worked quietly in California trying to understand the raging debate over whether a jetport should be built near the northern boundary of Everglades National Park, in Florida. The conservationists and the land developers flew across the country to talk to us. We discovered that both groups had a working hypothesis that if one was for something, the other ought to be against it. But, in fact, there was an outcome *both* had reason to fear, on different grounds, and so could unite to prevent: the drainage of the interior. The water flowing slowly southward through the inland region containing the jetport site not only prolonged the wet season in the Everglades, establishing critical rhythms for the entire ecosystem, but also played an essential role in protecting coastal fresh water supplies, so that coastal land development and inland drainage were incompatible over the long term. The developers, in particular, had not appreciated the scale of planning that limits to fresh water resources demanded. By emphasizing the opportunity costs of a future of unplanned regional development, our report (along with several others) led state and federal officials to reappraise the value of "undeveloped" land. A consequence of that reappraisal has been the creation by the federal government of the Big Cypress Swamp Water Conservation Area, a development which, at the time of our study two years before, had seemed unwise both to the conservationists and to the developers—extravagant to the former, an infringement on property rights to the latter. Another consequence has been the relocation of the jetport 30 miles to the northeast.[8]

A similar reappraisal of the value of undeveloped land occurred as a consequence of the 1970 National Academy of Sciences summer study of plans to extend Kennedy International Airport into Jamaica Bay. The attitude of public officials to the Bay as a recreational resource, other than for bird watching and nature study, was well expressed by the head of the New York City Department of Parks and Cultural Affairs when he said, "If you put your foot in that water, it will come out bones." Accepting the assumption that the objectives of an extensive program of water pollution control already underway would be fulfilled, our group emphasized a possible future in which Jamaica Bay would be intensively used by the people of Brooklyn and Queens for water sports. By suggesting modifications of a plan for the extension of regional subways that would permit access to the Jamaica Bay shore, and by suggesting locations and estimating costs of shoreline beaches, we were able to help those involved in the future of the area to imagine new alternatives. A consequence of such altered perceptions has been the redesign of the Gateway National Recreation Area: it now includes the shore of Jamaica Bay, where previously the boundary had been drawn at the water's edge.

The moral of these two stories, for me, is that no group of analysts, however constituted, should ever imagine that their work—whether it focuses on the "science" of a dispute or its politics—can proceed apart from the debate, for it always becomes part of the debate. As Laurence Tribe observes in his essay, "any analysis must become part of the process it has helped to shape." This is the classic conundrum of the observer and the observed embodied in Heisenberg's Uncertainty Principle, and it assures that the work of the analyst of land use disputes will have consequences —in the unfolding of that dispute and other disputes. I would rather commend to analysts the assumption that *everyone* is listening and will go on listening. Like Lord Keynes, I would expect that "madmen in authority, who hear voices in the air, are distilling their frenzy from some academic scribbler of a few years back. . . . Soon or late, it is ideas, not vested interests, which are dangerous for good or evil."[9]

C. What We Should Hear Before We Say the Discourse Is Good Enough

Once the quantitative analysis is so located that all interested parties are served, the discourse might just begin to sound quite different. I cannot imagine more than a fraction of the themes we might hear; but I would regard the appearance of straight talk about any of the following to be a signal that a transition had occurred.

1. Bigshots. The sheer size of Tocks is a source of excitement. For those who might build the dam, it is a challenge to their organizational and technical skills—a challenge that enlarges their perception of themselves. Correspondingly, the high stakes (the expenditure of about a billion dollars is in the cards for dam construction, new sewer facilities, and additional transportation access) spur on the activists in the conservation groups, who believe that only victories on issues like Tocks will ever get a fair hearing for their broader philosophical analysis of modern society.

Stopping a project this big will thrill a conservationist in a way not very different from the way building it will thrill a Corps engineer. It is debatable, under the circumstances, whether big projects get wiser consideration than little ones. Big projects may get a first-string team, so that there is less carelessness and foolishness, but they also engender momentum for its own sake—the drive for victory rather than compromise.

To like being a bigshot is pretty human. Yet it dampens the enthusiasm for taking seriously the packages of single-purpose projects, the half-dam and quarter-dam strategies, which (as discussed in section II) are often meritorious alternatives to the one big structure. Building a set of wing dams that jut partway across the river and create swimming areas in the slow-moving water behind them doesn't count for much today. A discourse grown sensitive to bigness will display creativity in the scoring and rewarding of intermediate accomplishments.

2. Little Guys.   The local residents live with the uncertainty that the stalled discourse has brought. Most would prefer a decision either to build or not to build, relative to a decision to postpone deciding. This fact confounds the kind of analysis usually regarded as optimal: one that keeps the options open.

The Corps has been acquiring the land where the lake and the National Recreation Area are to go. Some of the people who have had to sell to the Corps are bitter about the procedures by which these sales have been accomplished, and they are persuasive when they argue that there are not enough built-in safeguards to protect them. Given the fact that much of the fuel for the opposition to the dam comes from these bitter residents, the current procedures for land acquisition are clearly suboptimal.

It used to be presumed that if people want to live on flood plains, the government should not stop or even dissuade them; a proper role for government was simply to assure that those living in flood plains were aware of the risks. Flood-plain zoning generally goes much further, setting the government in systematic opposition to the determined risk taker. It may be that the characteristics of this silent confrontation could be usefully illuminated.

The urban poor in the inner cities of Newark, New York City, and Philadelphia who do not have cars will not be able to travel the 50 to 75 miles to the National Recreation Area, whether river-based *or* lake-based, if there is no public transportation. What subsidies, if any, would be required to provide such public transportation at prices these groups could afford? If subsidies of this sort prove to be necessary, those who make their approval of any particular form of the project conditional on its serving the needs of the urban poor ought to insist that the project incorporate such subsidies. There is a risk of self-deception if this problem remains unexamined.

The recreation area, politicians sense, will be used by different groups if it is built around a river or around a lake. What characteristics differentiate these two groups? A careful answer to this question would clarify the currently muddled perception of winners and losers.

3. Wilderness.   Men can now move mountains, melt icecaps, turn rivers around. Their power to assault leads to competing images of nature as victim and nature as ward. In either case, nature is politicized.

Doing nothing has now become a judgment: the act of not implementing a technology to modify a natural phenomenon is politically and morally different from the act of leaving nature alone at a time of innocence. Apparently, Fidel Castro, following a devastating hurricane over Cuba, went on the radio to accuse the United States *not* of seeding the hurricane in a way that went awry, but of *failing* to seed the hurricane, knowing that it would hit his country.[s]

Suppose a decision is made not to build the dam, and the following year an immense crack develops in the Kittatiny Ridge, rocks begin to tumble into the valley, the river becomes plugged, and a lake builds up behind the plug. Does the Corps restore the navigable waterway?[t] That the river should have standing in such a decision seems appropriate.[10] But if I were the guardian for the Delaware, I would be perplexed. I would not want my ward to drown Port Jervis and other human settlements on her banks. I would expect to see some abridgement of her prerogatives. Why should I assume that my river is a savage? Might not a river *like* the idea of being helpful to man? It is not obvious to me that the end result of an enlargement of rights must be an enlargement of selfishness.[u]

The problem of rocks falling into the river was posed in a discussion between dam builders and dam stoppers at a university, a setting that permits some of the usual rules of discourse to be

---

[s]I owe the story, as well as the basic thought in this paragraph, to Edith Brown Weiss.

[t]The Corps of Engineers, in its environmental impact statement, considered the possibility of taking the *dam* apart at a later time. The two relevant paragraphs are extraordinary enough to merit full quotation:

> With the exception of a large permanent rock face at the left abutment, occupation of the area by the project facilities does not in general constitute an irreversible or irretrievable commitment of resources.
>
> The major resource commitments are less enduring and of restorable character. In areas of local protection works the natural stream banks will be lost and replaced with flood walls and levees. The corridor of relocated U.S. 209 due to grade adjustments requiring cut and fill represents an artificial land modification. These features could be removed and the area completely restored to its pre-project uses, should future generations find that such removal and restoration could serve some greater public economic or social good. The construction of the basic dam embankment although very massive does not preclude its alteration or removal. While truly a major undertaking, this change could be made for a compelling (and as yet unknown) future need.

[u]As Laurence Tribe argues in his essay, "recognizing rights in a previously rightless entity is entirely consistent with acknowledging circumstances in which such rights might be overridden. . . ." My point goes a bit further: it is that recognizing rights does not preclude imposing responsibilities.

suspended. I look forward to the day when it is usual to have more open, more self-critical, even more playful discourse. I do not argue on grounds of efficiency alone; I rely on more than the enhanced potential for resolution of conflict. Such arguments from efficiency are not self-evident; if one knows one's neighbors better, one may want *less* to compromise with them. Improvements in discourse can be better justified in terms of higher ends than the instrumental one of "solving" the problem at hand. The new discourse would manifest a fuller expression of the diversity of preferences and emotional commitments of the participants. It would enhance the sensitivities of both participants and bystanders to the complex, tragicomic process of self-definition a culture goes through when it seeks to resolve any of its hard problems. It seems worth pursuing for its own sake.

NOTES

1. Jack McCormick and Associates, *An Appraisal of the Potential for Cultural Eutrophication of Tocks Island Lake* (U.S. Army Corps of Engineers, September 1971).

2. Thomas H. Cahill, "The Potential for Water Quality Problems in the Proposed Tocks Island Dam Reservoir," in G. E. Schindler and F. W. Sinden, eds., *The Tocks Island Dam, A Preliminary Review* (Save the Delaware Coalition, 1973).

3. Water Resources Engineers, *Lakeco: A Model of a Reservoir* (December 1972), and *Ecologic Simulation—Tocks Island Lake* (February 1973).

4. Wapora, Inc., *Tocks Island Lake: Techniques for Water Quality Management* (1974).

5. For a qualitative description of the state of the art, and a glimpse at the magnitude of current effort, see G. J. Eicher, "Stream Biology and Electric Power," *Water Power* (June 1973): 211–218.

6. *The Flooding River*, by Lincoln Brower, made in 1972 and available from John Wiley & Sons, New York.

7. See the *Report on the Comprehensive Survey of the Water Resources of the Delaware River Basin*, Appendix W, "Recreation Needs and Appraisals," House Document 522, 87th Congress, 2nd Session (1962), p. W-18.

8. See "The Everglades: Wilderness Versus Rampant Land Development in South Florida," in John Harte and Robert H. Socolow, *Patient Earth* (New York: Holt, Rinehart and Winston, 1971).

9. J. M. Keynes, *The General Theory of Employment, Interest, and Money* (New York: Harcourt Brace and World, 1964 ed.), p. 383; originally published in 1936.

10. The seminal essay on this subject is Christopher D. Stone, "Should Trees Have Standing?—Toward Legal Rights for Natural Objects," *Southern California Law Review* 45 (2):450–501. He was anticipated in some respects by Dr. Seuss (Theodor Seuss Geisel), *The Lorax* (New York: Random House, 1971).

❋ Chapter Two

The Tocks Island Dam Controversy*

Irene Taviss Thomson

Tocks Island does not appear on most maps of New Jersey. Nor is the protracted controversy over whether to build a dam there likely to put Tocks on the map. There have been no real heroes or villains involved and no national monuments at stake. The size of the project, the number of people affected, the scale of effects, and the emotions generated by the Tocks Island Dam controversy are not nearly as dramatic as those relating to the Alaska pipeline, for example. But many of the same issues appear in microcosm, and the story is of interest for what it reveals about environmental decision making in the current climate of opinion. From the time that the dam was first proposed in 1962 until the Delaware River Basin Commission decision in 1975 to ask Congress not to appropriate funds for its construction, over 50 studies of the dam had been undertaken. A review of the thirteen-year history of the Tocks controversy may help shed light on the problems of reconciling competing values and interests and on the complexities of policy analysis.

I. THE SETTING

The controversy can be starkly rendered: should a dam be built to provide some flood control, increased water supply, electrical power, and a new recreation facility, at the expense of destroying the local communities, interfering with natural processes and scenic beauty, and possibly provoking ecological damage? From different perspectives, the central issue has been variously defined as a matter of preserving vs. destroying a natural environment; economic growth vs.

*This chapter relies heavily on the work of the Princeton University research group that is reported in the companion volume, Boundaries of Analysis., no growth; recreation for the masses vs. maintenance of an elite preserve.

The parties to the decision have had to juggle a multiplicity of costs and benefits, both tangible and intangible. In some cases, of course, the interests of a politician's constituency may dictate a clear answer. It is not surprising, for example, to find a congressman from New York State opposed to the dam because of the costs to his farming constituency of measures to control or purify nutrient runoffs that could be expected to flow into the Tocks Island Lake. It is equally understandable that some New Jersey officials opposed the dam because the recreation facility would have entailed costs for New Jersey—for road building and a host of additional services—that would have benefited principally New York and Pennsylvania residents. Nor is it surprising to find the Corps of Engineers in favor of building the dam; building dams is, after all, what the Corps does.

But not all the political actors had ready-made positions available to them and the cast of characters involved to some degree in the Tocks dispute was quite large. It included the Delaware River Basin Commission (DRBC), the Army Corps of Engineers, the National Park Service, Congress (especially the Public Works and Appropriations Committees), the State Departments of Environmental Protection, the Federal Council of Environmental Quality, the Environmental Protection Agency, a variety of environmental and public interest groups (especially the Environmental Defense Fund and the Save the Delaware Coalition), industry (especially power companies, water supply companies, and members of the fishing, real estate, farming, and tourist industries), local residents, and a large number of state and local officials. Not all of these groups maintained a unitary position concerning the dam. The National Park Service, for example, housed both pro- and antidam factions, as did the New Jersey Department of Environmental Protection. In March 1974 the staff of the DRBC recommended that the dam be constructed. In August 1975, the DRBC Commissioners voted to have Congress deauthorize the project.

As studies of the costs and benefits of the dam proliferated, the desire to respect nature and preserve its diversity seemed to serve as the dominant force behind the analyses undertaken by groups opposed to the dam, while the values of efficiency, growth, and economic security underlay the analyses of dam proponents. The values of the latter group have a long tradition and a well established place in American society, while the values of the former have only recently begun to gain support. It is in part because of this divergence that an issue such as the Tocks project takes on significance. For those who are trying to establish a new principle—in this case to make respect for nature an acceptable value—each occasion for decision takes on aspects of a crusade. Listen to the language used:

> Concerned citizens all over the country are watching Tocks Island. The question here is no longer whether the old pork barrel brand of politics shall prevail. This is an issue of national magnitude, in which the little people who care will have their day. It marks the dawning of a new day, when the long-range effects on the environment must be measured, understood and evaluated before the shovel is turned, not after.[1]

What is being conveyed here is that: (1) "politics as usual" can no longer be sustained; (2) we are "little people who care"—that is, we are ordinary citizens fighting against powerful and entrenched bureaucracies and interests; and (3) we are not irrational nature lovers, but are seeking to make certain that long range environmental considerations are given their due. Explicitly, this is a call for a turning point in environmental decision making. Implicitly, it is also a defense against the image of environmentalists as a small elitist group who care more about rivers and fish and trees than about the exigencies and realities of human life.

The crusading element is absent, by and large, in the literature on the other side of the Tocks controversy. It has behind it the full weight of economic efficiency and high technology. There is much appeal in the multipurpose project—a dam that can protect against floods, provide water and hydroelectric power, and serve as the basis for a new recreation area near several densely populated cities. Since the 1930s the rationale for building dams has been that they serve many purposes: they induce regional development, reduce poverty, and become part of a larger, coherent structure of regional river basin planning.

Perhaps less obvious, but equally potent, is the traditional American appeal of technology. The idea of a "technological fix" for solving social problems may have been articulated only fairly recently, but the practice has long been characteristic. In a country where labor was scarce, land and resources plentiful, and mobility and economic growth highly valued, technology was developed and used to a greater degree than elsewhere. It was only natural, when problems developed, to attempt to find technical solutions. Surely it is easier to change technology than it is to change men's practices and institutions. Building a dam to provide water is easier than asking men to conserve water; building a dam to control floods is easier than asking them to move away from the flood plains or, in Robert Socolow's intriguing proposal, to accept the risks involved.

Environmentalists and others are now challenging this pattern. They argue that social change, however difficult, is possible—that social decisions can ordinarily be reversed, whereas many technological decisions are essentially irreversible. The river cannot be undammed; its ecosystem cannot be restored to the status quo ante. Within this broader context lie a host of social and technical issues that no analysis can completely untangle, such as: What kind of regional development is desirable? Should government respond to the recreational desires and tastes of the people or, as seems implicit in Laurence Tribe's and Robert Dorfman's essays, attempt to uplift them? What will be the long range economic consequences of the decision not to build the dam?

In an ideal world, where decision makers were democratic philosopher-kings and analyses incorporated all the subtleties that Laurence Tribe describes as possible in principle, the road from analysis to decision would be a relatively smooth one. But in a world where models are imperfect, knowledge incomplete, the public interest undefined, and decision makers often parochial in the extreme, the bumpy road of pluralism and what Charles Lindblom has called "muddling through" may well be preferable (and are, in any event, unavoidable). In the Tocks case, one set of analyses undertaken by dam proponents—the Corps of Engineers and the Delaware River Basin Commission—was challenged by another set of analyses done by opposition environmental groups. In the end, a more "objective" analysis authorized by the Congress served the purpose of propelling a decision, even though its findings may not have been crucial to the decision.

II. HISTORY OF THE PROJECT

In 1955, residents along the Delaware River and its tributaries experienced the worst floods in the history of the basin. The loss of lives and massive damages led to a renewal of interest in the possibility of building a dam. The idea was not a new one. Indeed, 1740 has often been noted as the date of the first proposal to erect a dam on the Delaware, and in 1933 the Army Corps of Engineers had studied the feasibility of a dam at Tocks. Spurred by the floods, Congress in 1956 authorized the Corps to restudy the Delaware River Basin and appropriated $2 million for the purpose. In December 1960 the Corps completed its Comprehensive Survey of the Water Resources of the Delaware Basin, which included the recommendation to build a dam on Tocks Island. This eleven-volume study, known as House Document 522 and released in 1961, has served as the principal basis of evaluation since that time, though numerous updates and changes have been made.

The affected states—New Jersey, New York, Pennsylvania, and Delaware—began to organize to deal with basin problems as early as 1939. In 1961, the Delaware River Basin Commission (DRBC) was created as an interstate agency whose five commissioners are the governors of these states and the United States Secretary of the Interior. In 1962, the DRBC adopted the plan devised by the Corps, and congressional authorization for the Tocks project was given in the Flood Control Act passed that year.

The earth and rock-fill dam to be built at Tocks Island, approximately five miles above the Delaware Water Gap, was to be 160 feet high and 3,000 feet long. It would flood 10,000 acres of land in addition to the 2,525 acres now covered by the existing stream; during temporary storage of flood waters, an additional 6,000 acres would be flooded. In 1962, the project was expected to cost an estimated $98 million in direct federal funds. Changes in design and in construction requirements coupled with inflation brought the estimated cost up to $400 million by 1975.

If flood control was the initial impetus for the Tocks project, nature soon provided a second purpose. During 1961–65, the area was struck by a severe drought, and maintenance of an adequate water supply took on considerable importance. The dam was to provide approximately 980 cubic feet of water per second. The original plan also included use of the dam to generate hydroelectric power. Congress subsequently authorized the construction of a pumped-storage facility at Tocks by private power companies, subject to approval by the DRBC and the Federal Power Commission. An estimated 70 megawatts of hydroelectric power would have been produced if there were no pumped storage plant, 1,300 megawatts if there were.

The fourth and final component of the Tocks project became one of the main elements in the controversy. This was the establishment of a recreation area at the Tocks site, using the lake created by the dam as a base. The lake was to run for 37 miles from Tocks Island to Port Jervis, New York, with a width of less than 3,000 feet through most of its length. The total recreation area would cover some 72,000 acres. In 1965, Congress authorized the Delaware Water Gap National Recreation Area (DWGNRA), to be run by the National Park Service. The language of that authorization tacitly assumed the existence of a dam; hence the Corps maintained that the dam and recreation area were inseparable. The National Park Service argued that they were indeed separable and that a river based recreation plan could still be implemented if no dam were built.

When the Tocks project was first authorized, it appeared to have widespread appeal. The only significant opposition came from local residents who were to be displaced. Some 600 of them filed a class action suit against the project in 1965, but the case was dismissed on the ground that the government had not consented to being sued. In 1968, when the power companies proposed using Sunfish Pond, near Tocks Island, as the upper reservoir for the pumped-storage facility, public opposition resulted in a campaign to "Save Sunfish Pond." This pond is a glacial lake situated at the top of the Kittatinny Mountain Ridge and approachable via the Appalachian Trail. The DRBC succumbed to this pressure, and another site for the reservoir was chosen. Apart from this minor episode, environmental groups seemed favorably disposed toward the project, largely because they saw it as an alternative to the growing commercial development of the area. The dam and associated recreation area were perceived as a way to prevent the kind of unpleasant sprawl and destruction of natural beauty that had taken place in the nearby Pocono Mountains area.

It was only as further studies were undertaken and the secondary effects of the dam were exposed that environmental groups came to oppose the project. Opposition seemed to become effectively mobilized only in 1971, when the Corps issued its environmental impact statement. From that time onward, the opposition gained momentum as governors, senators, and congressmen turned against the project in an environmentally conscious climate. For many of the dam's opponents, the argument was turned around. Far from protecting the area against unwanted growth, the dam came to be seen as encouraging industrial and residential development by providing more water and power and bringing tourist and commercial development along with the recreation facility. Certainly the vision of a recreation site initially planned for 9.4 million visitors annually did little to discourage such fears. The adverse secondary effects of the project that generated concern included traffic and other congestion, waste disposal problems, the unpleasant effects of seasonal drawdowns, possible lake eutrophication, and damage to fisheries. The destruction of the last sizeable free-flowing river in the East, the disruption of local communities, the destruction of at least some life forms in the area, and the inundation of a picturesque and historic valley became important rallying cries.

Both the Corps and the National Park Service began buying land in the area in 1965. Land acquisition, preparatory planning, and various analytic efforts continued through the 1960s, even though funding cutbacks during the Vietnam War delayed the necessary appropriations. In 1970, Congress ordered construction of the dam to begin as soon as approval was granted by the Council on Environmental Quality (CEQ). The Corps issued its legislatively required Environmental Impact Statement in 1971, but the statement was met by criticism from the Council and by a demand for revisions.

By this time, various opposition groups had been mobilized and became vociferous. New Jersey had a new governor, William Cahill, who had not yet taken a stand on the dam. His approval was considered necessary even though the DRBC Commissioners had approved the dam earlier. At the end of 1972, Cahill announced his opposition to the dam until seven specified conditions were first met. Further environmental impact studies raised serious questions about eutrophication of the lake, and the project remained in limbo.

In an effort to force some resolution of the controversy, Congress appropriated $1.5 million for a new study of the Tocks project in August 1974. These funds were to be used for "an impartial comprehensive analysis, including alternatives, and review of the project." The investigation was to be completed and "a final and definitive recommendation" was to be submitted to Congress by August 1975. Senator Clifford Case of New Jersey and others who were instrumental in arranging for the congressional appropriation had initially sought to fund a study that would deal exclusively with the question of eutrophication and related environmental issues. Various pressures operated against this approach, however. Budgetary constraints, for example, ruled out the possibility of a CEQ study, and jurisdictional politics within the Congress ruled out the possibility of an EPA study.

While the Congress was deliberating over who should do the study in the summer of 1974, the New Jersey Department of Environmental Protection acquired a new head, David Bardin, who was eager to see the DRBC undertake such a study. Bardin's office secured the cooperation of the Governor's office and in July, the DRBC Commissioners, prodded by New Jersey, unanimously adopted a resolution asking Congress for $1.5 million for a study. In August, Congress appropriated the money, but allocated it to the Corps of Engineers. The DRBC was unable to receive the funds directly because under existing laws Congress cannot appropriate money for the DRBC unless the funds are matched by the four states involved.

Congress attempted to smooth over this difficulty by authorizing a study "under the direction of the Corps of Engineers and in cooperation with the Delaware River Basin Commission."

The proposed study became a subject of debate, nevertheless. Dam opponents expressed the fear that the results of the study would reflect the biases of its sponsor, the Corps of Engineers, irrespective of who received the contract to do the study. Because they effectively shortened the duration of the study, the inevitable delays in establishing the study's precise mandates and in assigning a contract for the work further fueled the fears and suspicions of dam opponents. Two prestigious research groups—the National Academy of Sciences and the Rand Corporation—declined to bid on the study because of the short time period allowed to complete it. In an attempt to ensure impartiality, Governor Brendan Byrne of New Jersey named a ten-member Citizens Advisory Board to monitor the progress of the study.

While some residents in the areas most directly affected by the dam preferred any resolution of the controversy to the prolonged uncertainty, others formed a new coalition in opposition to the dam. They were anxious that the local opposition to the dam be taken into account in the final decision; they were also concerned about what would happen to the thousands of acres of land already purchased by the government in the event of a decision against the dam. Their fear was that big private developers might buy the land that individuals could not now afford to purchase. Organized labor, on the other hand, expressed irritation with the congressional authorization of yet another study. They urged prompt construction of the dam in order to provide work for the unemployed.

The announcement of a new study thus became the occasion for increased lobbying by both supporters and opponents of the dam. At the same time, Governor Byrne indicated publicly that he was opposed to construction of the dam unless the study were to turn up some new "compelling reason" for it. Earlier, in May 1974, Malcolm Wilson, then governor of New York, indicated that he was opposed to the dam if New York would have to pay for the waste treatment facilities needed to prevent pollution of the Tocks Island Lake, or if New York's dairy and poultry industries were likely to be harmed by the project.

After some time, two New York City consulting firms were given the contract for the study: URS/Madigan-Praeger, and Conklin and Rossant. They released the separate sections of their report to the public as they were completed, and a series of public hearings was held to discuss the findings. The six-volume, 3,600-page, fifteen-pound final report was duly produced and noted. The report assessed the costs of various alternatives, but took no position on whether the dam should be built. In essence, the consultants' study concluded that the various alternatives to the dam would be financially costlier, but less costly to the environment. The Corps of Engineers responded predictably by announcing that its analysis of the study showed that the dam should be built at once. Equally predictably, the environmentalists attacked each segment of the report as it appeared as biased.

When the DRBC Commissioners met in August 1975 to make a decision about the Tocks Island Dam, they apparently did not pay much attention to the consultants' study. Before the vote, Russell Train of the Environmental Protection Agency and Russell Peterson of the CEQ had urged a vote against the dam. In the final DRBC vote, which was to ask Congress not to appropriate funds for construction of the Tocks Island Dam, the Interior Department abstained and Delaware joined New Jersey and New York to outnumber Pennsylvania's lone favorable vote. Although there may have been some element of suspense before the vote was actually cast, most of the participants had made their positions known considerably earlier. New Jersey and New York had all but officially committed themselves in opposition to the dam. Governor Sherman Tribbitt of Delaware had announced in advance that he would join the majority in the DRBC, since Delaware was minimally affected by the Tocks decision. Governor Milton Shapp of Pennsylvania had long been one of the staunchest supporters of the dam. Although it voted to reject the dam, the DRBC approved the establishment of a national recreation area to be administered by the National Park Service around the free-flowing Delaware River. On this issue, both Pennsylvania and Delaware abstained, while the Interior Department joined New Jersey and New York in approval.

III.   THE ISSUES

Cahill's Seven Conditions

Before examining the controversy in detail, a look at the seven conditions that former Governor Cahill of New Jersey felt should be met before he would approve construction of the Tocks Island Dam will help to pinpoint some of the issues. Two of these conditions related to zoning authority. They were (1) that New Jersey and Pennsylvania enact legislation authorizing state control of land use in the flood plains, and (2) that state and local units of government in New Jersey be given authority to control land use in the primary impact area. These legislative changes were deemed by Cahill to be desirable in any event, although they would be more necessary if the dam were built.

A third condition was aimed at reducing congestion at the recreation site and minimizing the strain on the affected local communities. It stipulated that the recreation plan be scaled down to accommodate a maximum of four million visitors a year (rather than 9.5 million) and that adequate camping facilities be constructed in order to minimize commercial development. In a visit to the area before announcing his decision, the governor had met with a large number of local officials who were worried about their inability to cope with a large influx of visitors. Not only would they be plagued by inadequate facilities for fire and police protection, hospital and ambulance services, and solid waste disposal, but they would suffer loss of tax revenues because of federal acquisition of lands. Two other conditions were thus designed specifically to help reduce these problems: (1) the DRBC was to authorize the construction of a dispersed sewage plant system, and (2) the federal government was to consider payments to local units of government to compensate for loss of tax revenues as a result of federal acquisition of lands.

A sixth condition imposed by Governor Cahill was that the federal government provide substantial funding for the construction of new highways. This demand stemmed from the results of a study commissioned by the New Jersey Department of Transportation in 1969. The study, by Edwards and Kelcey,[2] assessed new transportation needs on the basis of the recreation area plans set forth by the Corps in House Document 522 and by the National Park Service in its 1966 "Master Plan," as well as on the basis of findings of an earlier study cosponsored by New Jersey and Pennsylvania on the expected impacts on the region surrounding Tocks.[3]

The Edwards-Kelcey study concluded that the required road network in New Jersey would cost an estimated $680 million. A similar study commissioned by the Pennsylvania Department of Transportation concluded that an estimated $40 million of road construction would be required on the Pennsylvania side. The magnitude of these sums—greater than the cost of the dam itself—and the potential impact that these roads would have on the local area became powerful arguments against the dam, and the failure of the Corps even to consider such important secondary effects served substantially to discredit their analysis.

The seventh condition—the demand that adequate control of nutrient runoffs be assured so as to prevent or diminish eutrophication of the lake—had broader significance than the first six, which can be construed as largely addressed to the parochial interests of New Jersey.

Eutrophication

The problem of potential eutrophication of the lake became one of the largest stumbling blocks to acceptance of the Tocks project. The principal objection voiced by the CEW to the Corps' Environmental Impact Statement was its inadequate treatment of this problem. As a result of CEQ prodding, the Corps commissioned a study of eutrophication. This study, the McCormick Report, concluded:

> Even though the data are meagre ... they suggest strongly that the proposed reservoir, in light of current conditions, will experience rapid eutrophication. Frequent algal blooms, aesthetically objectionable shoreline conditions, a low sports value of fisheries, and other symptoms of degradation of the aquatic environment can be expected.[4]

The report noted that the usual reservoir management techniques to retard eutrophication are most appropriate for water supply reservoirs and could not be employed in this case because the lake was to be used for recreation and hydroelectric power as well as water supply. Instead, it recommended sewage treatment to remove 98 percent of the phosphorous in the nutrient runoffs, a water quality monitoring network to provide baseline data and to assist in the formulation of control techniques, and the establishment of a comprehensive water quality control program for the Upper Delaware River Basin. "Such a program," the McCormick Report noted, "will require the cooperation of local, state, interstate, and federal governing bodies and their agencies."[5] After noting the various recommendations of this study, the Corps' Environmental Impact Statement concluded that the problem of eutrophication is "subject to control" and that controls "can be implemented during the construction program and in advance of stream closure."[6]

Securing the cooperation of the governmental bodies involved was not a simple matter, however. In 1972, Russell Train, then chairman of the CEQ, sought assurances from the Governors of the affected states that they would cooperate to meet several sewage treatment requirements. He also requested assurance from New York's then Governor Nelson Rockefeller that the area above the reservoir that was not included in the regional waste treatment plan receive top priority for federal and state funds for phosphate removal. Rockefeller indicated that he could not provide such assurances. Nor did the other Governors consent to Train's requests.

It is neither unusual nor surprising that statewide needs take priority over regional projects. Elected officials do not operate from a regional perspective.[7] Since regional water problems are not a primary concern to the Governors, they must ask themselves questions of a different sort. Why should New Jersey Spend money to build roads that would benefit primarily New York and Pennsylvania residents? Why should New York spend money to control nutrient runoffs for a lake in New Jersey and Pennsylvania? The DRBC staff, on the other hand, is concerned with regional water management, and not with problems of land use, transportation, or recreation. Both they and the Corps of Engineers argued that since the Tocks project represented a large proportion of the overall Delaware River Basin Plan, elimination of that project would necessitate a rethinking of the whole plan and might jeopardize future water resources development in the region.

The multipurpose nature of the Tocks project complicated all the analysis and debate in much the same manner that treatment of the eutrophication problem in Tocks Island Lake was rendered more difficult by the multiple uses of that reservoir. Robert Socolow has suggested that insisting on multipurpose projects tends to discourage a search for new and imaginative solutions to problems. The central criticism directed against the Corps' analysis of the Tocks project has been its failure to examine single-purpose alternatives adequately: there are other means for generating power and providing water; there are nonstructural alternatives for flood control; and the park can be built without the lake. The position of the Corps has been that, taken together, all four benefits are best and most efficiently provided by the dam, and that other ways of fulfilling these needs would generate problems of their own.

The URS/Madigan-Praeger and Conklin and Rossant study (1975)—which did examine single-purpose alternatives—concluded that the lake would indeed be eutrophic. Efforts to control the pollution would be costly and might actually destroy the source of the pollution, the poultry industry in the upstate New York area. The study also supported the claim of the environmentalists that unsightly mudflats would develop around the periphery of the lake during annual summer releases of reservoir water. These mudflats would lead to erosion, which could in turn result in pouring sediment into the reservoir, thereby further increasing the pollution. Thus the use of the lake as a source of water would greatly interfere with its recreational use.

Eutrophication was considered a more serious problem for the recreational use of the lake than for the water supply. The 1975 consultants' study found that the reservoir water could be treated and made safe for drinking. Therefore, for those like Governor Shapp whose principal interest in the dam lay in its water supply and flood control purposes, the eutrophication problem remained of minor concern. In a letter to the *New York Times* published on September 11, 1975—after the DRBC vote—Governor Shapp contended that "many Pennsylvania lakes are used for recreation and have a greater inflow of pollutants than that projected for the proposed Tocks Lake, yet there is no danger to the users."

Recreation

In the Corps' cost-benefit analysis, the largest proportion of total benefits from the Tocks project was attributed to recreation—43.7 percent. This figure was derived by multiplying the estimated number of annual visitors by $1.35 per recreation day and subtracting from this $1.35 times the estimated number of annual visitors to the area in the absence of the project. The $1.35 valuation was adopted from Senate guidelines; it is clearly an arbitrary figure, and probably something of an underestimation even in its own terms since the guidelines prohibit escalation to reflect cost of living increases. Nor does it take into account the aesthetic quality of the recreation site or the degree of crowding or privacy. The estimate of the number of visitors to be accommodated seemed almost as arbitrary. Citing a Senate mandate to develop the recreation potential to its "highest and best use," the Corps estimated that 9.4 million people could be accommodated.

Little analysis was done to support this claim, and after first having adjusted it upward from 7 million, the Corps scaled the number down to 4 million in response to Governor Cahill's stipulation about maximum annual use. Project opponents were quick to point out, however, that the revision was accomplished simply by substituting the first stage of an originally planned two-stage project, which also called for building four sites instead of ten, so that the revised plan neither reduced the density at any site nor precluded eventual expansion. Another figure that was questioned was the number of current annual visitors to the area. The Corps used 183,000, but estimates range as high as 1.25 million, and a 1969 review of the project by the General Accounting Office which pointed out this discrepancy helped to support suspicions that the Corps had seriously overestimated the benefits of the project as a whole.

What is the import of all these numbers? All parties to the dispute appear to agree that open space and recreational facilities are badly needed in the area. Tocks Island is approximately 50–75 miles from New York City, Philadelphia, and Newark. The question, then, becomes facilities of what kind, where, and for whom. The number of current visitors would seem to be a most inadequate basis for assessing potential recreation benefits since the very decision to build a dam would, as Laurence Tribe has pointed out, affect the preferences of nearby populations and hence change the demand on which the visitor-day estimates are based. Furthermore, the type of analysis used by the Corps naturally leads to building high density mass recreation facilities because the benefits increase in direct proportion to the number of users. This produces a "more is better" psychology that is not confined to the analysis alone, for once one announces the prospect of a recreation area designed to serve large numbers of people in the crowded Northeast, opponents have a difficult time proposing alternatives that would accommodate fewer people. They feel constrained to argue that their own schemes can satisfy almost as many people as could the dam.

The aim of the alternative plans is to reduce the crowding, noise, transportation, and other problems attendant upon densely populated beaches along the lake and to provide instead a "natural system plan" in which the free-flowing river and surrounding scenic lands would offer more dispersed recreational activities. Proponents of the alternative approach argue that crowded beaches would provide little respite from urban conditions. Furthermore:

> Since the same recreational experience can be provided at any reservoir, lake, pond or pool closer to the cities, it is difficult to see how the expenditure of transportation resources can be justified for this purpose. . . . The land that would be flooded by the reservoir is the most usable in the Park. The long-distance bicycling, the camping, picnicking, hiking, canoeing, riding, fishing, etc. that could be provided on this land and river, and that would be precluded by the reservoir, can be denser in people per square mile without palpable crowding than can the boating (especially if it includes water-skiing) that would be provided by the reservoir's surface. The planned massive swimming beaches are dense, to be sure, but they are not appropriate to the Park in any case. Moderate swimming beaches, in keeping with the setting, would not require a reservoir. They could be provided in many places along quiet stretches of the river without severe disruption of the landscape. . . . A park without a reservoir, based primarily

on bicycling on the unflooded flatlands, and canoeing on the unflooded river, could be used much of the year. Thus a given yearly visitation could be achieved with less crowding in such a park. Among other advantages, spreading the load over the year would ease the transportation problem.[8]

This plan replaces images of Coney Island with images of a natural river and open countryside, available for multiple uses to large numbers of people. In the words of another proponent: "The native scene, complete with fishing on a flowing stream, canoeing over the river rapids, hiking past Sunfish Pond on the Appalachian Trail, deserves Federal sponsorship. Such a park would be less expensive than a dam and reservoir and of far more value to the public over a longer period of time."[9] The problem is: which "public"? Would the people who flock to Coney Island or Sandy Hook be likely to come to the Delaware Water Gap to canoe and fish and hike? Also, given the distances involved and the absence of ready access by public transportation, is it likely that the facility would be used by the really poor people of New York, Philadelphia, and Newark?

Such questions have by and large been evaded. The Corps came close to facing the issue, though obliquely. In discussing the possibility of the DWGNRA without the dam, it argued that this alternative would not satisfy the recreation objective:

> While there is a natural beauty inherent in a wild, free-flowing river, this development would nonetheless provide recreation opportunity for only a limited number of people. . .The paramount reason for this is that a large body of water such as Tocks Island Lake is a proven attraction in a recreational project of this type. Visitor affinity for water recreation generally runs two to one over land activities.[10]

For the environmentalists, turning a natural river into a beach by creating a lake and surrounding it with trucked-in sand has much the same flavor as replacing real trees with plastic ones, an enterprise that is much discussed in Laurence Tribe's essay for this volume. It represents a future in which the natural is replaced by the artificial, the esthetic minority is sacrificed to the culture of the masses, and the enduring and historical give way to expedient and transient concerns. Applying Tribe's argument in this context, large crowded beaches give rise to demands for more of the same as people's experiences shape their choices. If a "taste" for natural beauty is to be developed, people must be exposed to it. Hence, leave the river free-flowing, preserve the natural environment, and open up the surrounding countryside.

But there is another problem involved. True preservation of the environment often requires the exclusion of people; a wilderness cannot remain a wilderness if it is subjected to any substantial human use. Currently, only 5 percent of the river shoreline in the project area is open to public access. Construction of the DWGNRA, even without the lake, would drastically alter this situation. There would be more people, noise, dirt, cars, roads, and the inevitable realities of commercial development. Proponents of the natural system plan have argued that all of these effects would be far more serious if the lake-based park were implemented. But the environment would be substantially altered under either plan.

Environmental groups have by no means been of one mind on the Tocks project. United in their opposition to the dam, they have differed on the issue of the DWGNRA and how large it should be. In recognition of what might be termed the "people problem," some have opposed any recreational facility in the area. Tawdry commercial development of the area is, of course, anathema to all, although the best means to prevent it do not seem clear. In an ironic postscript to an environmentalist victory, a man who had been instrumental in saving Sunfish Pond wrote a letter to a local newspaper in which he complained about the toll that people take on nature. He noted that, on a recent visit to the pond, he found the hitherto peaceful area strewn with litter and wracked with the noise of motorcycles. He wondered whether it had been worth "saving" the pond.

The Corps of Engineers has argued that without any intervention, farm lands are being turned into second homes, permanent homes, and recreation facilities. The conversion of land use to recreation purposes "has been accomplished by commercial developers with, in many cases, scant regard for environmental degradation."[11] Thus, "future developments within the project boundary would eventually eliminate a large portion of the present wildlife habitat and impair the natural character of the region. Presently there are no uniform standards effectively governing regional development."[12] But "this trend toward environmental degradation will be reversed with develop- of the project due to. . .attendant orderly development of the surrounding lands."[13] Moreover, the Corps maintained, since the beaches would not constitute the whole of the recreation area, less densely populated land would be available for other recreational uses.

It is an interesting commentary on the ambiguous status of the value of economic growth today that Governor Cahill of New Jersey felt constrained not to oppose economic growth outright despite his personal predilections and the concerns of local officials, while the Corps of Engineers, traditionally a champion of growth, felt constrained to adopt a somewhat muted tone. The Corps takes note of the fact that "pre-project commercial tax revenue will eventually double and employment opportunities increase. Through flood control 4,000 acres of land previously undeveloped or providing low economic return would be made available for economic development or for improved land uses."[14] It goes on to say:

> Many of the region's residents, particularly those in the low income areas, on the Pennsylvania fringe, will welcome better socio-economic conditions as an improvement. The provision of short-term services for visitors, such as daily and weekly sleeping accommodations and eating establishments, will stimulate the local economy and create jobs for many residents. Many permanent and seasonal residents will be distressed over the loss of the existing and predominantly rural and scattered commercial development pattern. Careful zoning controls and other local regulatory measures will be needed to prevent future commercial development serving the visiting public from occurring in areas outside the DWGNRA and the lake project, in a way that conflicts with sound regional land use plans.[15]

The Corps seems to be saying that although economic growth is good, it does have some unpleasant consequences, which can be controlled through appropriate regulations. In this instance, the Corps minimizes the difficulties of land use and zoning controls. Yet it continued to question the feasibility of such measures for providing nonstructural alternatives to flood control.

It is of interest that a majority of the residents in the local communities most directly affected by the project opposed construction of the dam. In referenda in two of the four affected counties (Monroe in Pennsylvania and Warren in New Jersey), voters opposed the dam by margins of three to two, but supported the establishment of the DWGNRA by two to one.

The 1975 consultants' study of the Tocks project noted the high current and future demand for recreational facilities in the region. It concluded that the New York area, for example, needs additional facilities for nearly two million more swimmers than can now be accommodated on an average summer Sunday. As alternatives to the Tocks facility, it proposed the expansion of the state parks and the construction of numerous swimming pools in parks closer to population centers. The consultants also suggested that the stretch of the Delaware that would have been dammed could be designated a part of the country's Wild and Scenic Rivers System to preserve it in its natural state. The DRBC voted to take advantage of the federal purchase of more than two-thirds of the 72,000 acres that had been proposed as a recreation area, and recommended the acquisition of the remaining land for the establishment of a park. Governor Byrne has announced that plans are being drawn up to protect Warren and Sussex counties from the overdevelopment that might otherwise arise in the wake of the development of a national recreation area.

Flood Control

The Corps of Engineers had attributed 10.8 percent of the total benefits of the Tocks project to flood control. The proportion was small largely because the Delaware flood plain between Tocks and Trenton is sparsely populated. Yet the benefits as estimated by the Corps assumed largely uncontrolled growth and development on the flood plain, and were calculated on the basis of the damages that would be prevented on property that increased in value because of flood control. This ignored the possibility that zoning and insurance schemes might be adopted to retard growth on the flood plain. In fact, several communities have successfully adopted such measures, and a study by the Environmental Defense Fund found that since 1955, the population and the number of structures along the mainstem flood plain had either remained stable or decreased slightly. By contrast, development along the tributaries—which would not have been protected by the Tocks dam—had increased considerably.[16]

Opponents of the dam have often pointed out that the dramatic 1972 floods in Rapid City, South Dakota caused 235 deaths and much damage, despite the presence of a flood control dam fourteen miles away. The dam offered no protection because the rain fell in an area below the dam. Furthermore, they argue, the construction of a dam often sets in motion a vicious circle in which the protection afforded by the dam encourages further development along the flood plain and hence increases the damage potential. The increased damage potential in turn may generate pressures for further flood control structures. The argument of dam opponents is that because of the essential unpredictability of floods, a dam alone provides insufficient protection. It must be supplemented by zoning regulations, insurance plans, flood warning systems, and emergency relief provisions. Then, if such measures are implemented, and considering the environmentally undesirable consequences of the dam, one should reconsider whether the dam is necessary at all.

The Corps argues that in the absence of a dam, the land and properties downstream of Tocks would still be subject to flood damage and potential loss of lives. Insurance plans serve to redistribute the economic loss, not to do away with it. It is unrealistic to expect effective flood-plain zoning because of the high degree of regional development and the multitude of political subdivisions. Furthermore, relocation of industrial structures would be extremely difficult.

Because of uncertainties in predicting the frequency and location of floods, similar difficulties arise in the design of both structural and nonstructural flood control devices. In any event, to afford maximum protection, a combination of both means of control is usually considered desirable. Although both sides to the dam argument accept this in principle, the Corps maintains that structural controls are of primary importance, while the Environmental Defense Fund, for example, contends that "reservoir construction should be considered only when it is clear that flood plain management measures are inadequate for the task."[17] Essentially, the Corps is intent upon preventing floods, whereas the environmentalists are concerned with minimizing flood damages. Environmentalists appeal to the need for adapting to nature and refraining from building structures that cause environmental and ecological disturbance.

Until recently, federal funding priorities heavily favored structural means of flood control. This is beginning to change, however, perhaps due in part to the work of the President's Task Force on Federal Flood Control Policy. The Task Force found that despite the large sums of money devoted to flood control, losses due to flooding have continued to increase each year, largely as a result of increased development of the flood plains. Such findings, which point to the inaccuracies in flood prediction that render structural flood control measures inadequate, would seem to undercut the assumptions used in the Corps' cost-benefit analysis. In calculating the flood control benefits, the Corps had included the increased revenue to be derived from greater utilization of the land in the flood plains. The Task Force findings suggest that such land use is unwise and ultimately unproductive economically.

The 1975 consultants' study recommended flood-plain zoning as being considerably cheaper than the dam and producing "comparable" results. Flood-plain zoning could have the additional effect of reducing the growth of such cities as Trenton, Camden, Philadelphia, and Wilmington, by halting the riverside location of new manufacturing facilities, which have traditionally sought readily accessible water transportation. By contrast, the dam would have served to spur riverside development downstream. Many proponents of the Tocks Island Dam still contend that flood control protection will be inadequate without the dam. Governor Shapp, for example, argues that Trenton and Easton, Pennsylvania could be "wiped out" in a flood. He further maintains that without more water, Philadelphia will not be able to retain its industry.

Water Supply and Power

Of the total benefits of the Tocks project as assessed by the Corps of Engineers, 33.8 percent are attributable to water supply, 11.7 percent to hydroelectric power. With water supply as with flood control, the alternatives proposed by the environmentalists entail social and economic changes. For in addition to suggesting different methods for increasing water supply, they contend that various means of reducing demand must also be implemented. Once again, the main concern is to break the cycle of ever-increasing technological interference with nature. In line with their desire to adapt to nature, environmentalists also argue that people can tolerate some fluctuations in water supply in order to avoid the environmental costs of constructing a dam to provide an assured and constant supply.

As enunciated by a study prepared for the Environmental Defense Fund, the basic argument was that demand must be reduced in any event, lest the Tocks Island Dam become inadequate to supply the ever-increasing demands. On the other hand, if programs to reduce demand do not succeed, there would be adequate time to construct the dam because the establishment of the DWGNRA preserves this option.[18] Not all environmentalists share this position. Some maintain that a more careful study of water needs invalidates some of the assumptions made by the Corps and the DRBC. Once these assumptions are corrected and other sources of water supply are taken into account, they argue, the dam can be shown to be unnecessary.

The initial analysis of water supply and demand set forth by the Corps in House Document 522 has been superseded by an analysis done by the DRBC in 1971. According to DRBC estimates, the most significant increase in future demand for water will arise in connection with the installation of electric power plants that consume water for cooling. Second, there is a demand from the state of New Jersey to divert 300 million gallons of water per day (mgd) out of the basin to its heavily developed northeastern section. Finally, the Tocks Island Dam would satisfy the demand for minimum flow of 3,000 cubic feet of water per second (cfs) to be sustained at Trenton even under drought conditions. This amount of fresh water flow has long been considered necessary (it is one of Socolow's "golden numbers") to prevent salinity from exceeding a tolerable level. The figure of 3,000 cfs at Trenton is also used as the basis for the pollution abatement program adopted by the DRBC. These three sources of demand have constituted the principal justification for building a dam for water supply. Projected water needs for municipal, industrial, and agricultural uses are insignificant by comparison.

Opponents of the dam have questioned the accuracy of these estimates. They note that, although the DRBC analysis relied on quite different analytic methods and sources of demand, the demands it projects for the next 50 years almost exactly matched the supply that the Corps of Engineers had initially estimated would be made available by the dam. Adding to the resulting suspicion is the fact that estimates of the need for cooling water have been based on studies done by the power companies. A consortium of eight utility companies operating in the Delaware Basin had projected a need for seventeen new power generating plants and nine expanded plants by 1986.[19]

The DRBC estimates for cooling water requirements assumed a somewhat less rapid growth. Nevertheless, the rate of increase involved would quickly consume much of the additional water provided by the dam. Environmentalists argue that such heavy use of water would be self-defeating and must be regulated. They contend that power plants should not use fresh water for cooling. The use of dry cooling towers and the siting of power plants either offshore or in brackish water lower in the estuary are suggested as alternatives, although offshore siting may produce problems of a different sort and dry cooling is expensive.

The diversion of 300 mgd of water to northeastern New Jersey is by no means a foregone conclusion. Although environmentalists have suggested means of providing this water without the dam, the status of New Jersey's request for this diversion remains uncertain. The request has only recently been made formal and the DRBC has not yet granted its permission. The number itself is of uncertain origin. One investigator traces it to a 1955 study that cited 300 mgd as the amount of water northeastern New Jersey would need by the year 2000 from all new sources. That study reported that the entire amount could be obtained from within the state if necessary, but recommended that one-third be taken from the Delaware.[20] The 1975 consultants' report made no firm estimate of what the demands for additional water would be. It did conclude that high-flow skimming could produce the 300 mgd for as little as 8¢ for each 1,000 gallons.

Environmentalists have proposed that a system of high-flow

skimming could be used to provide the necessary water. During periods of high stream flow the water would be pumped from the Delaware and stored offstream in an already existing reservoir, Round Valley. It has been estimated that this technique would provide enough water to satisfy New Jersey as well as maintaining the minimum 3,000 cfs flow at Trenton, and that the cost to New Jersey would be lower than its share of the Tocks Island Dam water supply costs.[21] Environmentalists have also proposed that water supply could be increased by conjunctive use of high-flow skimming and ground water, or by the use of ground water from the Pine Barrens aquifer. The Corps has countered this suggestion by noting that although the environmental effects of a potential overuse of ground water are uncertain, ground surface subsidence and salt water intrusion have resulted in some regions of the country.

The need to maintain a 3,000 cfs flow at Trenton has also been questioned. It is alleged that there has been insufficient analysis to demonstrate that any such level is needed. Many environmentalists, however, are willing to accept this figure for purposes of debate, largely because existing capacities do not fall very far short of it. Their argument is quite straightforward:

> The DRBC asserts in its Water Resources Program that as soon as the Beltzville dam on the Lehigh River is on-line, . . . it will be possible to guarantee a flow of at least 2700 cfs at Trenton. Moreover, a profile of the 25-year drought (low-flow conditions occurring on the average once in 25 years) determined by the Federal Water Pollution Control Administration shows that the flow during such a drought drops below 3000 cfs only for the single month of lowest flow (September) and then only to about 2700 cfs. Thus, with a flow assured which only drops below 3000 cfs (on a monthly average basis) perhaps once in 25 years and even then is deficient by no more than about 10%, an adequate baseline flow has been provided.[22]

The added protection of 300 cfs that would be assured by the dam is viewed as a feeble justification for the project. The 1975 consultants' report found the likelihood of saline instrusion to be extremely small. It noted that if the peril should ever arise, however, an alternate water supply for Camden could be developed from ground water in the Pine Barrens and elsewhere and that Philadelphia's intake pipes could be relocated.

In addition to challenging the need for a dam to augment the water supply, environmentalists have proposed a number of measures to conserve water and restrict demand. These include altering the pricing and rate structures for water, repairing faulty plumbing, recycling waste water for industrial purposes, alternative means of cooling for power purposes, and some changes in consumption habits. By virtue of a 1954 Supreme Court decision, New York City can take 800 mgd of water from the Delaware. It has been estimated that, if the city were to repair its leaks, at least 300 mgd could be released down the Delaware instead of being diverted—in other words, more than the amount that New Jersey would like to take.[23]

In comparison with the debates surrounding the recreation, flood control, and water supply functions of the dam, power generation has been of minimal concern. Because alternative sources of power are clearly available, the issue has not been seen as salient by either the proponents or the opponents of the dam. The fact that the small conventional hydroelectric power facility would be constructed by the government while the pumped-storage plant would be built by the utility companies has drawn some attention to the long standing issue of whether power should be in public or private hands. For the rest, environmentalists have cited the usual alternatives—especially the use of gas turbines instead of pumped storage—while dam proponents have noted that these alternatives also have environmental costs.

The 1975 consultants' report concluded that the power companies need no additional capacity until the mid 1980s. Even then they may require peak capacity only briefly. By the early 1990s, such new technologies as battery storage fuel cells and compressed air could probably handle any growth in the demand for power.

IV. ENVIRONMENT, GROWTH, AND ANALYSIS

The issue of ecological damage never became a significant component of the Tocks controversy. Ecologists had expressed concern that changes in salinity caused by regulation of the river flow would lead to "simplification" of the environment of the Bay—that is, to a decrease in the number of species inhabiting the ecosystem. The consequence would be a reduction in diversity and possible impairment of the stability of the ecosystem. Environmentalists acknowledge that "at present, the full range of such consequences . . . cannot be spelled out in detail." Nevertheless, they argue, "one should be prepared to assume that such typical consequences of simplification could be among the environmental effects of further flow regulation and increased depletive use."[24]

To the environmentalists, uncertainties about the precise effects dictate a stance of caution toward intervening with nature. But the position of some environmentalists goes beyond a concern for the possible negative effects upon people of altering the natural environment. Their fundamental premise is that nature should be left unaltered unless and until it can be shown that interference is truly necessary. In effect, it is a plea to treat nature itself as something like an endangered species. Thus, in response to the environmental impact statement issued by the Corps, the New York Department of Environmental Conservation argued that "the loss of free-flowing stream listed as an adverse effect should be given much more weight. The real significance of this loss is the fact that this is the last major unimpounded stream in the East."[25]

The Department also proposed that:

> A more detailed discussion should be presented on the alternative of no action. This would require a projection of the future environmental setting if the project is not accomplished. A discussion should also be presented of the alternative(s), if any, investigated with environmental objectives as the sole purpose. . . . It should be noted that each generation is a trustee of the environment for succeeding generations and any proposal which would narrow the range of choices of future decision makers should be avoided.[26]

In what may be an unprecedented statement, the Corps has seen fit to note that "the construction of the basic dam embankment although very massive does not preclude its alteration or removal. While truly a major undertaking, this change could be made for a compelling (and as yet unknown) future need."[27] Obviously this concession, unusual though it may be, offers a rather impractical suggestion. Dams are not temporary structures. The values of diversity and reversibility were simply not given weight in the analysis.

In the initial phases of the Tocks debate, the boundaries of analysis were too narrowly drawn, as the failure to consider such issues as access roads and eutrophication amply demonstrate. Many of the inadequacies of analysis are rooted in the real and perceived responsibilities of the institutional actors. As has been noted, neither the Corps nor the DRBC has responsibility for land use or transportation. Hence the ways in which construction of the dam would impinge on such matters were not given serious consideration in their analyses. Fragmentation of responsibility was also manifest with respect to problems directly related to the narrowly defined functions of the agencies. For example, the DRBC did not explore the possibility of using the aquifer in the Pine Barrens in southern New Jersey as a source of water supply for northern New Jersey largely because the Pine Barrens water is outside the Delaware Basin. The agencies that do have jurisdiction—the United States Geological Survey, the New Jersey Bureau of Water Resource Planning, and the Corps of Engineers—did not attempt to coordinate their activities. As a result, the Geological Survey thought that the Bureau of Water Resource Planning was investigating the biological aspects of the use of the aquifer, while the Bureau thought the Geological Survey was doing so.

If fragmentation of responsibility has sometimes contributed to the poor quality of analysis, so has excessive coordination. The congressional directives that mandated uniform discount rates and the use of $1.35 per visitor-day as the measure of recreation benefits introduced an unwarranted arbitrariness into the analysis. Both those figures might have been different had they been derived in the course of analysis of this particular project. One may wonder, for example, whether the number of visitors used by the Corps in its analysis might have been smaller if the guidelines had allowed the figure used to compute recreation benefits to reflect cost of living increases.

Whatever the difficulties involved in arranging for a satisfactory allocation of responsibilities, it would seem that, if the relatively intangible environmental values are to receive their due, they must become the responsibility of some institution or agency. This appears to have been taken care of, at least partially, through the mechanism of the Environmental Impact Statement. The requirement that this statement be carefully reviewed by affected parties and approved by the CEQ has put the brakes on undertakings that might have had apparently untoward environmental consequences. In the Tocks case, it may be recalled, potent environmental opposition was mobilized only in response to the Environmental Impact Statement itself. Although some have argued for far more direct and powerful means of incorporating environmental sensitivity in analyses and decision making, both the difficulties involved in doing so and the limited and tentative agreement on the importance of such values militate against much more rapid or dramatic changes.

NOTES

1. Michael Frome, "Preface," *The Tocks Island Dam: A Preliminary Review* (Philadelphia: Save the Delaware Coalition, 1973), p. x.
2. Edwards and Kelcey, *Approach Roads Study, Tocks Island Region*, Part I, April, 1969, Part II, March 1971.
3. Robert R. Nathan Associates, *Potential Impact of the DWGNRA on Its Surrounding Communities* (Washington, D.C., February 1966).

4. Jack McCormick and Associates, *An Appraisal of the Potential for Cultural Eutrophication of Tocks Island Lake* (Devon, Pa., September 1971), p. 92.

5. *Ibid.*, p. 96.

6. Department of the Army, Philadelphia District, Corps of Engineers, *Tocks Island Lake Environmental Impact Statement* (Philadelphia, October 1971), p. 4–4B.

7. In this connection, see Bruce Ackerman, Susan Rose Ackerman, James W. Sawyer Jr., and Dale W. Henderson, *The Uncertain Search for Environmental Quality* (New York: The Free Press, 1974).

8. F. W. Sinden, "Planning, Recreation and Transportation for the DWGNRA," in *The Tocks Island Dam: A Preliminary Review*, op. cit., pp. 125–126.

9. Michael Frome, *op. cit.*, pp. ix–x.

10. *Tocks Island Lake Environmental Impact Statement*, op. cit., pp. 5–3 – 5–3a.

11. *Ibid.*, p. 3–6.

12. *Ibid.*, p. 6–1.

13. *Ibid.*, p. 4–1.

14. *Ibid.*, p. 3.

15. *Ibid.*, p. 4–5.

16. Laurie Burt and Leo Eisel, *Flood Control and the Delaware River* (East Setauket, N.Y.: October 1973).

17. *Ibid.*, p. 119.

18. M. Disko Associates, *New Jersey Water Supply: Alternatives to Tocks Island Reservoir*, prepared for the Environmental Defense Fund (West Orange, N.J., October 1973).

19. Tibbetts, Abbott, McCarthy, Stratton, *Water Resources Study for Power Systems, Delaware River Basin*, March 1972.

20. See Frank W. Sinden, "Water Supply" in Harold A. Feiveson, Frank W. Sinden, and Robert H. Socolow, eds., *Boundaries of Analysis: An Inquiry into the Tocks Island Dam Controversy*, (Cambridge, Mass.: Ballinger, 1975).

21. See Smith Freeman, Edwin Mills, and David Kinsman, "Water Supply and the Tocks Island Dam," in *The Tocks Island Dam: A Preliminary Review*, op. cit., pp. 4–17.

22. Freeman, Mills, and Kinsman, *op. cit.*, p. 10.

23. See Sinden, "Water Supply," *op. cit.*

24. Smith Freeman and Werner Schmid, "Depletive Use of Delaware River Water," in *The Tocks Island Dam: A Preliminary Review*, op. cit., p. 20.

25. See *Tocks Island Lake Environmental Impact Statement*, op. cit., p. L–6.

26. *Ibid.*, p. L–2.

27. *Ibid.*, p. 7–1.

Chapter Three

Ways Not to Think About
Plastic Trees*

Remember these things lost;
    and under the vaulting roof of the cathedral
    burn a candle to the memory.[1]

Baudelaire's *Rêve Parisien* paints what is quite liter-
ally a still life—a dreamscape of a metallic city where
groves of colonnades stand in the place of trees and, in the
place of water, pools of lead.[2] More prosaic but no less unnerving
was the recent decision by Los Angeles County officials to install
more than 900 plastic trees and shrubs in concrete planters along the
median strip of a major boulevard.[3] The construction of a new box
culvert, it seemed, had left only 11 to 18 inches of dirt on the strip,
insufficient to sustain natural trees.[4] County officials decided to
experiment with artificial plants constructed of factory-made leaves
and branches wired to plumbing pipes, covered with plastic and
"planted" in aggregate rock coated with epoxy. Although a number
of the trees were torn down by unknown vandals and further
plantings were halted, the tale may not be over. For an article in
Science suggested recently that, just as advertising can lead people to
value wilderness and nature, so too it can "create plentiful
substitutes."[5] "The demand for rare environments is . . . learned,"
the *Science* article observes, and "conscious public choice can
manipulate this learning so that the environments which people learn
to use and want reflect environments that are likely to be available at
low cost. . . . Much more can be done with plastic trees and the like
to give most people the feeling that they are experiencing nature."[6]
    While so explicit an acknowledgment of the acceptability of
artificial environments may be unusual, the attitude it expresses
toward the natural order is far from uncommon. Increasingly,
artificial objects and settings supplant those supplied by nature.

*This essay was originally written for the present volume but has appeared in
a more preliminary, but more fully documented version, in *Yale Law Journal* 83
(1974): 1315–1348.

Durable Astroturf replaces grass in football stadiums and around swimming pools. Guests at the Hyatt Regency Hotel in San Francisco walk among more than 100 natural trees growing in the twenty-story lobby but listen to recorded bird calls broadcast from speakers hidden in the tree branches. And Walt Disney World offers a multitude of visitors what one *Newsweek* writer described as "a programmed paradise."[7]

I do not focus on Astroturf and the plastic trees of Los Angeles as harbingers of our most urgent environmental problems. Although the long term prospects in this regard are probably more troublesome, I claim no imminent risk that we will too cleverly engineer ourselves into a synthetic hell. Quite apart from any such danger, I believe that such "nature surrogates" provide an illuminating metaphor through which to expose and criticize certain premises that underlie most current discussions of environmental thought, law, and policy.

While it might appear initially that nature surrogates would be antithetical to the ecological concern embodied in present environmental legislation and policy, a closer analysis leads to precisely the opposite conclusion. The perpetually green lawn and the plastic tree, far from representing the outcroppings of some inexplicable human perversion, are expressions of a view of nature fully consistent with the basic assumptions of present environmental policy. These assumptions, which are implicit in developing uses of policy analysis as well as in emerging institutional structures, make all environmental judgment turn on calculations of how well individual wants, discounted over time, are satisfied.

In this essay I seek to identify the roots and expose the inadequacies of this want-oriented perspective; I then tentatively outline the shape of an alternative foundation for environmental decision making and environmental law. The key to such an alternative foundation, I will argue, is to move beyond wants. I propose giving institutional expression to the perception that "nature exists for itself" by taking steps to recognize "rights" in natural objects, not as a way of broadening the class of wants to be aggregated by a utilitarian calculus, but rather as part of a structure for approaching a shared agreement about our responsibilities as persons—responsibilities to one another and to the world.

I. THE LIMITS OF ANALYTIC SOPHISTICATION: NATURE AND REASON IN THE SERVICE OF MAN

Despite occasional probes in less familiar directions, the emerging field of environmental law is being built on the basic platform of analytic sophistication in the service of human need. Statutes and judicial decisions typically mandate "systematic" and "interdisciplinary" attempts to "insure that presently unquantified environmental amenities and values may be given appropriate consideration in decision making along with economic and technical considerations."[8] Public interest challenges to decisions alleged to be environmentally unsound are diverted by the pressures of doctrine and tradition from claims about the value of nature as such into claims about interference with human use, even when the real point may be that a particular wilderness area, for example, should be "used" by no one.

A. Technical Capacities and Limitations

1. **Fragile Values.** From the start, the aspect of environmental policy analysis that has most concerned students of the matter has been the supposed difficulty of ever incorporating certain *kinds of values* into systematic analyses of environmental problems, whether in the service of legislators, of planning agencies, of litigators, of private enterprises, or of courts.[a] Variously described as fragile, intangible, or unquantifiable, these values have been widely thought to possess peculiar features making them intrinsically resistant to inclusion along with such allegedly "hard" concerns as technical feasibility and economic efficiency. In particular, those dimensions of a choice for which market prices do not exist have seemed to pose intractable obstacles to "objective measurement."

It does not take long to discover, however, that this emphasis on categorizing fragile values embodies a misleading formulation of the problem and an inadequate appreciation of the analytic capacities latent in the techniques under examination. To be sure, the aspirations of some policy analysts to an elusive "objectivity," the identity of their constituents, and the advocacy often expected of them by their clients, induce certain practitioners to overlook or understress a variety of values that might, in context, be characterized as "fragile." More specifically, insofar as analysis is intended to help a decision maker persuade others of the justifiability and wisdom of his choice, its usefulness in the absence of consensus as to

[a]In assessing the tendencies of contemporary thought with respect to analytic methods and their place in environmental policy, I am relying only in part upon the published literature. For my views on these matters have been shaped not only by such literature but also by the series of meetings and discussions sponsored by the American Academy of Arts and Sciences under the auspices of the National Science Foundation of which this collection and the companion volume are the result.

goals is predictably reduced whenever it does not at least appear to point "objectively" and unambiguously toward a particular alternative.

The users of policy-analytic techniques in advocacy situations are thus under constant pressure to reduce the many dimensions of each problem to some common measure in terms of which "objective" comparison seems possible—even when this means squeezing out "soft" but crucial information merely because it seems difficult to render commensurable with the "hard" data in the problem.[9] These tendencies are aggravated by the institutional and legal contexts in which analytic techniques are ordinarily used. Such techniques tend to be deployed as tools only by the individual combatants in policy conflicts; thus the only values consistently served are those strongly held by persons motivated and able to seek a policy analyst's aid—a circumstance likely to exclude values too widely diffused over space, or too incrementally affected over time, to be strongly championed by any single client of a policy analyst; values associated primarily with persons not yet in being (future generations); and values not associated with persons at all (for example, the "rights" of plants or animals).

Having said all this, however, one must concede that there is nothing in the structure of the techniques themselves, or in the logical premises on which they rest, that inherently precludes their intelligent use by a public decision maker in the service of these "intangible," or otherwise "fuzzy," concerns.[b] Despite what appears to be a widely held assumption to the contrary, all such concerns can in theory be incorporated in a rigorous analysis, either by using various market price or other numerical surrogates to value extra-market costs or benefits, or by the technique of "shadow pricing"—that is, qualitatively describing as best one can the contents of a constraint as intangible as natural beauty or procedural fairness or respect for future generations, and then calculating the tangible benefits that would have to be forgone if one were to insist that one's policy conform to the constraint described.

Thus, even in the relatively unsophisticated (by current standards) cost-benefit analyses performed to evaluate alternative levels of water quality improvement in the Delaware estuary, the enhanced swimming, fishing, and boating possibilities of a cleaner Delaware River were translated into dollar terms. The methods used in that translation were highly questionable in their ability to measure the

---

[b]This is not to say that the use of the techniques may not affect the values served by them. (This problem is explored in Part II A.)

economically relevant variables (that is, to measure how much prospective swimmers, fishermen, and boaters would willingly sacrifice before becoming indifferent between the enhanced opportunities caused by an improvement and the opportunities previously available to them),[10] and it is true that those variables themselves could not measure the value of enhanced water quality to future generations, or to the aquatic life that inhabits the estuary.

But an observer who believes that such values also matter could describe their significance in any terms that seem appropriate, and the analyst could then calculate how costly it would be to raise the water quality to the level demanded by the observer's description. Whether the sacrifice was justified by the values invoked would then have to be determined by whichever individuals or groups were responsible for making the choice in question. That their decision would be a difficult one reflects not any intrinsic weakness of the analytic methodology as applied to nonmonetizable values, but rather the universal difficulty of choosing among incommensurables—a difficulty that can be obscured but never wholly eliminated by any method of decision making.

It should be added as a qualifying caveat, however, that the tools of analysis are currently too blunt to be of very great use in this endeavor or in the discourse that surrounds it. If the analytic disciplines are truly to clarify the relations within and among values so as to identify otherwise unnoticed inconsistencies, and to show that some perceived conflicts are in fact illusory by inventing policies from which groups with apparently conflicting interests can all benefit, then the analytic fields, and the scientific disciplines which support them, must sharpen both their capacity to ask and answer probing and imaginative "what if" questions, and their capacity to understand and describe in some detail what each of the nonmonetary values significantly involved in a choice really represents.

Organizations engaged in environmental policy analysis are rarely able today to discover or to articulate the underlying character of the ecological and esthetic concerns (many of them essentially symbolic) that play so major a role in environmental disputes, or to design the models that would be needed to facilitate a thorough search of even mildly novel alternatives. It may be, as Murray Gell-Mann has proposed,[11] that we must therefore develop a new group of professionals sensitive to the sorts of values and issues that analyses currently tend to slight—diversity, balance, esthetic quality, reversibility, the claims of the future—and adept at modeling policy impacts in terms of such values. In studying a particular environmental case, such professionals might translate each of the relevant values or concerns into a parameterized constraint designed to show how costly the options for choice would be from the perspective of the value at issue. Thus, for example, a "distortion of natural landscape"[12] index might be studied to determine how slowly or rapidly the other costs associated with a project would rise if that index were constrained within lower and lower levels; and an "ecological diversity" index might be examined to ascertain what increments in various cost curves would result as one tightened the ecological constraint by forcing this index ever higher.

The curves generated by this sort of analysis will at times have a more complex structure than those typically assumed by analysts, especially those trained primarily in neoclassical economics. For example, most individuals would probably not trade breathing rights below a certain point for even limitless rights to pollute. And many persons—far from regarding such human capacities as eyesight, hearing, and physical mobility as all subject to continuous trade-offs to levels approaching zero—probably have preference orderings that display significant discontinuities, lexicalities,[13] and nonzero thresholds, which an adequate analysis would be forced to consider.[14]

Among the most serious of the difficulties the analyst would face—and it is a difficulty that economic analyses of "rights" have invariably overlooked—is that being "assigned" a right on grounds essentially reducible to arguments from efficiency with respect to the relevant cost curves might well fail to satisfy peculiarly human needs that can be met only by a shared social and legal understanding that the right (e.g., a right to breathe or to see) belongs to the individual because the capacity it embodies is organically and historically a part of the person that he is and not for any purely contingent and essentially managerial reason.[15]

However difficult the investigation of such ordering structures might be, and however complex may be the general task of defining the relevant parameterized constraints and generating the associated curves, the effort to move analysis in such directions should at least prove illuminating. And even before anyone is very good at the task of attaching shadow prices to varying levels of constraints as elusive as ecological diversity, the *attempt* to attach them rather than simply incorporating such constraints in an all-or-nothing fashion should lead to better decision processes, even if not better outcomes. Whether or not new professions must be developed in order to perform this sort of task sensitively, it seems clear that treating the problem as an inherent incapacity of analysis to incorporate the intangible can only retard the needed development of these important abilities.

2. **Conflicting Goals.** A second common formulation of the
limits of environmental analysis has centered on the alleged difficulty
of systematically dissecting problems characterized by a multiplicity
of partially or wholly conflicting goals. Analytic techniques can be of
virtually no use, it has at times been suspected, outside the few
situations (rarely encountered in the environmental field) where one
is optimizing a single, well defined objective subject to agreed-upon
constraints.[16] It is true that many analytic methods prove most
powerful in the single objective case and that various pressures tempt
both analyst and client, however misleadingly, to reduce all the
dimensions of a question to a common denominator (such as "net
benefits," as in the case of the Delaware estuary analysis) or at least
to smoothly exchangeable attributes. But the temptation is one that
has at times been resisted. The existence of that temptation, while
properly a source of caution in the application of analytic techniques
to environmental problems, cannot warrant a conclusion that those
techniques are useless, or even that they are invariably more
dangerous than helpful.

The approach of displaying a multitude of perspectives, with a
distinct objective function defined for each,[c] has often been proposed—sometimes vaguely, but occasionally in a quite unambiguous
and operational form.[17] Such techniques make it possible at least
to expose for intelligent debate the trade-offs involved in various
alternatives, and sometimes even to suggest formerly unconsidered
options that would "score" well in terms of all the perspectives
under examination. If techniques of this sort are augmented by
bureaucratic and organizational analyses that realistically take into
account the milieu in which policies are in fact made and carried out,
their predictive value—and hence, indirectly, their prescriptive value
as well—may prove to be considerable in environmental controversies, particularly when we understand more thoroughly than at
present the bureaucratic politics peculiar to organizations with
environment related responsibilities and the behavioral dynamics of
the situations they routinely confront.

3. **Means-Ends Fluidity.** Yet a third tentative hypothesis regarding the limits of analysis has been the possibility that, perhaps in

[c]An "objective function" is a rule that associates with each potential choice a
single mathematically determined value by means of which the choice can be
comparatively ranked with respect to a defined goal, objective, or attribute—
such as total cost to a particular individual or group, or risk of death to another,
or level of aesthetic enjoyment (however approximated) to still another.

environmental matters even more than others, most people lack clearly articulable ends and values at any given time and have only vague ideas about what they might regard as desirable or undesirable; such inchoate values are crystallized into distinct preferences or criteria of choice only through the concrete process of seeking means to attain them and gradually discovering what such means entail. There is no "spook . . . which posits values in advance."[18]

The fluid character of means-ends relationships has long been postulated, and I have elsewhere argued that it ordinarily describes the actual situation not only during the process of choice but in its implementation as well.[19] Indeed, I would hypothesize that most of the crucial environmental choices confronting industrialized nations in the last third of the twentieth century will be choices that significantly shape and do not merely implement those nations' values with respect to nature and wilderness. Such choices will do more than generate a distribution of payoffs and penalties to the persons affected in terms of their preexisting yardsticks of cost and benefit. Choices of this type will also greatly alter the experiences available to those affected, the concomitant development of their preferences, attitudes, and cost-benefit conceptions over time, and hence their character as a society of persons interacting with one another and with the natural order.

The hypothesis of such means-ends fluidity may, however, say little more than that the choice and implementation of means have some "feedback" effects upon the chooser's ends. Indeed, the fluidity hypothesis seen in terms of feedback effects renders systematic analysis all the more valuable as a means of bringing ends to light, and all the more essential inasmuch as wholly intuitive approaches to decision might overlook the means-ends complexity that a more rigorous investigation could help to illuminate.

The need again is not for an abandonment of rigor and precision but rather for its enrichment—this time by encouraging closer study of the range of psychological and sociological mechanisms, including self-perception and cognitive dissonance, through which the ends held by individuals and groups are shaped by the questions they ask, the intentions they form, the processes of choice they adopt, and the choices they in fact make. Even the most sophisticated analyses of environmental issues have been oddly oblivious to this problem of variable ends and shifting values,[d] in part no doubt because our

---

[d]Even those studies such as Wildavsky's "Political Economy" (supra) that recognize that goals are not "given" but emerge in the process of analysis and choice, strangely ignore the dependence of ends on the means actually chosen and implemented and on the experiences that result.

understanding of value formation is so rudimentary. But failing altogether to take this sort of dependence into account can only result in solving an unintended problem while leaving unsolved the problem initially put—rather like firing at a moving target that is connected to the marksman's arm without paying any attention to the link between the two.

Having considered the most serious technical obstacles to "good" environmental analysis and planning, one is forced to conclude that none of these obstacles need prove insuperable. Each calls for further research in preparation for more sensitive analyses and both greater creativity and closer vigilance in whatever environmental analyses are in fact conducted.

B. Ideological Boundaries

A final obstacle remains. Policy analysts typically operate within a social, political, and intellectual tradition that regards the satisfaction of individual human wants as the only defensible measure of the good, a tradition that perceives the only legitimate task of reason to be that of consistently identifying and then serving individual appetite, preference, or desire. This tradition is echoed as well in environmental legislation, which protects nature not for its own sake but in order to preserve its potential value for man.[20]

By treating individual human desire as the ultimate frame of reference, and by assuming that human goals and ends must be taken as externally "given" (whether physiologically or culturally or both) rather than generated by reason, environmental policy makes a value judgment of enormous complexity and significance. And, once that judgment has been made, any claim for the continued existence of threatened wilderness areas or endangered species must rest on the identification of human wants that would be jeopardized by a disputed development. As our capacity increases to satisfy those wants artificially, the claim becomes tenuous indeed.

Consider again the plastic trees planted along a freeway's median strip by Los Angeles county officials. If the most sophisticated application of the techniques of policy analysis could unearth no human want that would, after appropriate "education," be better served by natural trees, then the environmental inquiry would be at an end. The natural trees, more costly and vulnerable than those made of plastic, would offer no increment of satisfaction to justify the added effort of planting and maintaining them. To insist on the superiority of natural trees in the teeth of a convincing demonstration that plastic ones would equally well serve human desires may seem irrational. Yet the tendency to balk at the result of the analysis remains. There is a suspicion that some crucial perspective has been omitted from consideration, that the conclusion is as much a product of myopia as of logic.

II. BEYOND HUMAN WANTS: A NEW RATIONALE FOR ENVIRONMENTAL POLICY

What has been omitted is, at base, an appreciation of an ancient and inescapable paradox: we can be truly free to pursue our individual ends only if we act out of obligation, the seeming antithesis of personal freedom. To be free is not simply to follow our ever-changing wants wherever they may lead. To be free is to choose what we shall want, what we shall value, and therefore what we shall be. But to make such choices without losing the thread of continuity that integrates us over time and imparts a sense of our wholeness in history, we must be able to reason about what to choose—to choose in terms of commitments we have made to bodies of principle that we perceive as external to our choices and by which we feel bound, bodies of principle that can define a coherent and integrative system even as they evolve with our changing selves.[21]

To deny the existence of such bodies of principle is fashionable, but it is not inevitable. However obvious, it is worth recalling that most of the great philosophical systems of our own past—those of Plato and Aristotle, of Aquinas and the Scholastics, of Hegel and the Idealists—were grounded in the view that the highest purpose of human reason is to evolve a comprehensive understanding of mankind's place in the universe, not merely to serve as a detector of consistency and causality and thus as an instrument for morally blind desire. "The emphasis," as Horkheimer reminds us, "was on ends rather than on means."[22] It is only recently that the concept of reason as calculation without content became central in the West— that reason began to liquidate itself "as an agency of ethical, moral and religious insight."[23] Unless we are to remain in the shadow of that intellectual eclipse, we cannot simply assume that we must stand mute when confronting the utlimate question of whether we want our children, and their children's children, to live in—and *enjoy*—a plastic world.

The notion that nature in particular embodies values apart from its usefulness in serving man's desires is familiar even in the Western post-Enlightenment tradition. Kant, for example, taught that a propensity to exploit or destroy nonhuman and inanimate nature might violate a person's duty to himself.[24] Such utilitarian philosophers as Bentham advanced a related view, perceiving human obligations as extending to all entities capable of experiencing pleasure and pain.[25] And the contemporary philosopher John Rawls, after restricting his own theory of justice to the human sphere, went on to assert that it is "[c]ertainly . . . wrong to be cruel to animals and the destruction of a whole species can be a great evil."[26] Concluding that a correct conception of man's relation to nature "would seem to depend upon a theory of the natural order and our place in it," Rawls has exhorted metaphysics to work out a world view suited to this purpose, identifying and systematizing "the truths decisive for these questions."[27]

The task that Rawls thereby defined will not easily be accomplished, either as an intellectual matter or as an institutional one. From the perspective of a social order in which law has come to be justified either in purely formal, positivist terms (as the command of the recognized sovereign), or in terms of a projected tendency to maximize aggregate human satisfaction over time, or in terms of a contractarian conception of justice as fairness to other human beings, the elaboration of human obligations to nature is likely to appear idiosyncratic at best and incoherent at worst.

Although legislators and jurists might concede the appeal of an ecological or evolutionary theory that could suggest a conceptual basis for extrapolating beyond the perspective of human wants, they would undoubtedly resist efforts to incorporate any such extrapolation into a system of legal protection. The widely held view that law exists for the purpose of ordering individual wants in human societies, and for that purpose alone, may well prove an unassailable article of faith.

Given the obvious difficulty of progressing against the grain of such a faith, it seems appropriate to assess the importance of the task. How serious is the distortion occasioned by an entirely want-regarding vision? In precisely what ways—apart from the basic affront to freedom described earlier—is it troublesome to view nature solely in terms of potential for individual human satisfaction? In short, what's wrong with plastic trees, if that's what people really want?

A. The Distortions Implicit in a Want-Oriented Perspective

Theoretically at least, policy analyses and legislative provisions can be so calibrated as to be sensitive to, and then to accommodate, whatever values individuals are capable of discerning. Yet it does not follow, simply because all values susceptible to human perception may thus be formally "included" in our designs, that an institutional system or an analytic technique that relentlessly treats all such values as manifestations of individual human preference will prove satisfactory. To reach such a conclusion would require another premise: that the act of characterizing all values as expressions of such human preference or want will not affect their content or distort their perception. It is a premise that does not withstand scrutiny.

Saying that "nature" should be preserved only because of its beauty to its human beholders or its benefit to human users may risk burdening some natural places and phenomena with a peculiarly human insistence on attempted immortality: a canyon, like a person, may be entitled to a "natural" death. It may also risk exposing other places or creatures, no longer deemed lovely or productive, to a peculiarly human inclination to destroy once hallowed sources of disappointed expectation.[28] Moreover, the very process of treating all values as based on personal preferences results in a major shift of focus. Attention is no longer directed to the ostensible content of the value but rather to the fact that it is a more or less abstracted indicium of self-interest. Even if one ultimately chooses the same actions under such a shift of focus—something I have suggested is unlikely—one may well end with the feeling that one has chosen them not out of obligation or for their own sake, but because their opportunity cost in terms of one's range of personal desires was low enough, thereby distorting the meaning of the choice and of the actions chosen.

To offer a simple illustration, suppose a person feels an obligation to protect a wilderness area from strip mining. The initial perception of that obligation is likely to take the form of sympathy for the wildlife and vegetation that would be destroyed or displaced. Indeed, the perceived obligation may display at least the rudiments of an internal structure. Killing "higher" animal life may seem unjustifiable except for compelling reasons (e.g., to sustain, or to avert a direct threat to, human life); destroying plant life may seem improper if destruction can be avoided without "undue" cost. Certain categories of harm that might leave human civilization intact while threatening the global ecosystem as a whole—widespread radioactive contamination of the oceans, for instance—may seem wrong regardless of the strength of the countervailing human interest.

If the sense of obligation prompts the individual to undertake some concrete effort on behalf of the environment, such as making an adverse response to an environmental survey, initiating a suit to enjoin the strip mining, or advancing an argument in favor of preservation, a subtle transformation is likely to be occasioned by the philosophical premises of the system in which the effort is undertaken. The richly if inarticulately felt obligation will be translated into the flatter but more precise terminology of human self-interest. It may be said that future generations will be deprived of contact with wildlife; that the esthetic satisfaction of certain individuals will be diminished; that other recreational areas will become overcrowded. Proponents of environmental protection will, at best, couch their disapproval of human mistreatment of nature in terms of man's ability to satisfy his own wants.

While the environmentalist may feel somewhat disingenuous in taking this approach, he is likely to regard it as justified by the demands of legal doctrine and the exigencies of political reality. What the environmentalist may not perceive is that, by couching his claim in terms of individual human wants and personal preferences, he may be helping to legitimate a system of discourse that so structures human thought and feeling as to erode, over the long run, the very sense of obligation that provided the initial impetus for his own protective efforts.

This metamorphosis of obligation into hedonistic self-interest and personal preference ironically echoes aspects of Mill's utilitarian theory. Mill argued that the sense of moral obligation was a subjective feeling developed through learning and association from the primary responses of pain aversion and pleasure maximization.[29] He discounted the possibility that obligation, when perceived as an accretion of such responses, might ultimately lose its compelling force and dissolve into unmitigated self-aggrandizement; in Mill's view, the impulse toward conformity and other social pressures would insulate ethical feelings from any such reductionist tendency.[30]

However justifiable Mill's faith in the efficacy of communal reinforcement in the context of interpersonal obligation, such reinforcement clearly plays a less important role when the occasion of an ethical impulse is not a member of the human community but a natural object. Despite impassioned efforts by ecologists to suggest the contrary, the satisfactions of individual persons (and even of future human generations) are not invariably congruent with the interests of the natural order as a whole, even if such a congruence can be established as between individuals and the human communities in which they live. Indeed, individually or communally defined human wants may often be at odds with the primal ethical impulse—the sense of duty beyond self—that gives passion and conviction to many who see elements of the inviolable in nature. In this situation, communal reinforcement, far from impeding the transformation of ethical obligation into a category of self-interest, may actually accelerate the process.

To return to our example, once obligation has been transformed into a mere matter of personal preference, the tendency is inevitable to compare the value of wilderness with the value of strip mined coal in terms of self-interest. From there it is but a short step to an even more blatantly reductionist approach: in order to insure that the comparison is "rational," the two values will almost certainly be translated into smoothly exchangeable units of satisfaction, such as dollars. While certain discontinuities may still be recognized—destruction of all wilderness areas may not be deemed worth even an infinite supply of coal—they will tend to be gradually eroded by the pressure toward analytic uniformity.

The translation of all values into individualistic, want-oriented terms thus creates two distortions. First, an inchoate sense of obligation toward natural objects is flattened into an aspect of self-interest; second, value discontinuities tend to be foreshortened. It is important to emphasize again that these distortions do not follow as a necessary result from the theoretical premises of policy analysis. Although Aaron Wildavsky suggested in a 1966 critique that cost-benefit techniques structurally presuppose the individualistic premise that only personal preferences matter,[31] it is obviously possible to compute the costs of an activity in any terms one wishes or to impose whatever nonindividualistic or even nonhomocentric constraint is deemed important. There is nothing in the logic of analytic techniques (or, for that matter, the logic of interest identification that precedes legislative enactment) that limits the use of such methods to the tradition of liberal individualism in any of its diverse forms.

The distortions occur rather because the process of interest identification, as it is presently employed, interacts in a crucial way with the content of the interest being identified. The identification takes place in the context of a system of attitudes and assumptions that treat individual human want satisfaction as the only legitimate referent of policy analysis and choice. It is a system of attitudes and assumptions that begins by treating only human wants and needs as having moral significance and ends by collapsing such human interests into a mere aggregation of morally arbitrary individual desires and preferences.

These assumptions, and the desire for analytic clarity that accompanies them, together exert an enormous reductionist pressure on all values that would otherwise seem incommensurable with a calculus of individual human wants. Thus the distortion results not from a logical flaw in the techniques of policy analysis but rather from what I have elsewhere described as the ideological bias of the system in which such analysis is imbedded, a system that has come to treat the individual human will and its wants as the center around which reason as calculation must revolve.

B. The Roots of Our Current Posture

No one should suppose that this bias is a shallow one or that it can readily be eliminated. Its roots lie deep within the western philosophical and theological tradition. It is important, therefore, to describe briefly certain aspects of this tradition even at the inevitable expense of simplification. The dominant religious consciousness of preindustrial western societies, representing the confluence and culmination of strands that began at points as diverse as the Near Eastern salvation faiths and early Greek monotheism, is the consciousness of transcendence.[32] That consciousness characteristically perceives God as an other-worldly entity—one standing apart from, and above, the world. Genesis proclaims the sovereignty of God over the physical universe; it is but a small step to infer the dominion of man, as God's representative on earth, over all of life. In a seminal lecture delivered before the American Association for the Advancement of Science in 1966, Lynn White pointed to the Judaeo-Christian tradition of transcendence as the underlying basis for what he then perceived as our ecological crisis.[33] That thesis has been much criticized as overdrawn, but it deserves elaboration in the present context.

Any society whose dominant consciousness posits the radical dichotomy between God and world, between heaven and earth, and (in the individualized manifestations of these dualities) between soul and body, is apt to regard natural and social phenomena as entirely appropriate objects of human manipulation and will, at least insofar as humanity is viewed by that society as uniquely participating in the divine. So long as man is thought to stand apart from nature, and the universally divine in individual man apart from his more particular manifestation as a concrete social being, the manipulative stance toward the world of physical processes and social structures, expressed respectively through the media of "technology" and "public policy," is likely to prove invincible.[34] And, as Max Weber has argued, there exists a natural correspondence between manipulation as a mode of conduct and instrumental rationality—the rationality of matching means to ends—as a mode of thought.[35] If man is pilot of the lower orders, it is instrumental reason that charts his way.

The view that White's thesis was misguided rests on a facet of Judaeo-Christian theology whose centrality he failed to recognize. In *Summa Theologiae*, Aquinas argued that man excels all animals not by virtue of his power but rather by virtue of the faculty of reason through which he participates in the kingdom of heaven; White's account seemingly left no room within the Judaeo-Christian mainstream for a divinely inspired stewardship of the sort suggested by Aquinas and so eloquently realized in the thought of St. Francis. But, if this is its limitation, White's thesis becomes chillingly plausible in the period when the rise of science heralds the death of God. For once one accepts the Baconian creed that scientific understanding can only mean technological power over nature, one can no longer hope for inspiration from beyond;[36] once reason is no longer perceived as guided by the divine, it can no longer serve as master and must be relegated to the place of slave.[37] It is through this thoroughgoing secularization of transcendence that Hume's dictum—that "reason is, and ought only to be the slave of the passions"[38]—is fully realized; for when God is absent, the "grand manipulator" must move the world not according to values divinely revealed but in accord with ends ultimately private to each person and empty of intrinsic significance because not derived through any dialogue beyond the self.

In a classic reply to Sartre's heroic effort to find authenticity in this very emptiness,[39] Heidegger saw in that existentialist stance only the haunting spectre of the human will willing itself in the void.[40] The age inaugurated for philosophy by Kant and carried to its relentless conclusion by Nietzsche—the age of human will as the center of reality—seemed to Heidegger to lack a center, a point of reference from which the works of the will might be assessed. So it is that instrumental rationality, the shadow in human thought of the manipulative pose inherent in transcendent consciousness, is reduced to the endless striving after ever-changing ends that has come to characterize much of contemporary life. So it is that progress becomes a frenzied caricature of itself, and that human nature, itself but a part of the natural order properly subject to human will, becomes subject to alteration without moral constraint as Yeats's vision becomes reality: the center will not hold.

It is to the secularization of transcendence that we may most instructively correspond the transition from Aquinas and the Scholastics to moral theorists in the tradition of contemporary liberal individualism. Treating the work of John Rawls as representative, one may observe that the basic structure of his contractarian argument—which seeks justice and just institutions in the arrangements he claims rational persons would freely choose under a veil of ignorance as to the positions they will occupy in the world they are designing—presupposes an "individualistic conception according to which the best that can be wished for someone is the unimpeded pursuit of his own path, provided it does not interfere with the rights of others."[41] While this concept allows Rawls to elevate the sentiment of justice from its status in utilitarianism as a "socially useful illusion"[42] to an antecedent principle of social behavior, it does not directly implicate man's relation to nature. As Rawls admits, duties imposed on persons by the capacity of animals to experience pain and pleasure fall outside the ambit of any contractarian doctrine.[43]

In Rawls's system, the good is no longer to be derived from first principles by divinely inspired reason or by any rational faculty but is the contractual composite of arbitrary (even if comprehensible) values individually held and either biologically or socially shaped. As was implicit in Kant, reason must be silent when confronting the lonely task of commitment to the substantive ends and values themselves.

The structure of the Rawlsian argument thus corresponds closely to that of instrumental rationality; ends are exogenous, and the exclusive office of thought in the world is to ensure their maximum realization, with nature as raw material to be shaped to individual human purposes. Thus when Rawls posits that a correct conception of man's relations to nature depends upon "a theory of the natural order and our place in it,"[44] he calls for a moral conception of ecological obligation that cannot be formulated within the tradition of his own thought. For the premises of secularized transcendence deny the existence of anything sacred in the world and reduce all thought to the combined operations of formal reason and instrumental prudence in the service of desire. The only entities that can "count" in a calculus of end-maximization, whether utilitarian or contractarian, are those entities that possess their own systems of ends or at least the capacity to experience pleasure and pain,[45] and nothing outside the private ends and pleasures of such beings can come to the rescue of a philosophy devoted solely to their pursuit.

Nor would it be enough, ultimately, to broaden the reach of such a philosophy by somehow "averaging in" the wants of all sentient beings and then including the "wants" that inanimate objects might be expected to have if they had wants at all. As one wry observer has asked, "Why wouldn't Mineral King want to host a ski resort, after doing nothing for a billion years?"[46] If the endless emptiness of a want dominated conception is ever to be overcome, the need is to move beyond wants—*even nonhuman wants*—as the only source of policy.

C. The Alternative of Immanence

How such a need might be met is not easily imagined. No supposed eastern ethic of nature's wholeness and of man's place can simply be "willed" into being, and none would be likely to prove helpful in hard cases even if it could be thus commandeered. Similarly, those strands of our own legal, intellectual, and religious heritage that once seemed to point the way toward reason as an agent of moral illumination now appear as dust, the task of reassembling them into a coherent and effective fabric seemingly beyond our grasp. Despairing of anything better—frightened with Pascal by "the eternal silence of these infinite spaces" but unable with him to embrace God—we may be tempted to accept a perfected form of formal and instrumental thought as marking the perimeter of legitimate aspiration. In so doing we may, as long as we have the courage, recognize the futility of the pursuit after intrinsically empty ends to which we are thereby consigned.

It is worth asking, however, whether such stoic resignation is an inescapable corollary of our contemporary situation. I would not presume to offer anything like a definitive answer, but I will advance a tentative hypothesis. Just as the disintegration of reason detected by Horkheimer[47] has its roots in a religious transformation, so the reintegration of reason and moral perception may be augured by the dawning of environmental awareness in contemporary law and culture.

Recall the observation that environmentalists often feel disingenuous when they seek to rationalize their position in terms of a want centered calculus, even one that gives more than the usual weight to the interests of future human generations, one that takes an unusually risk-averse posture in assessing available options, or one that talks in the language of nonhuman as well as human "wants." Such environmentalists "want to say something less egotistic and more emphatic, but the prevailing and santioned modes of explanation in our society are not quite ready for it."[48]

Those modes of explanation are not *quite* ready, but it is hard not to observe a convergence of trends that suggests a growing sense in contemporary industrialized societies that there is in fact something sacred in the natural, a sense that Edward Shils has rightly argued can be wholly secular.[49] One sees such a notion, at the most romantic and mystical extreme, in the fond longing for an imagined past of an unmechanized, decentralized, nonhierarchical, antitechnological community of man in nature. One sees essentially the same notion, at the opposite pole, in the idea (closely related to "natural law") that modern science itself, and the unfolding structural truths it reveals about the natural order and the human condition,[50] can somehow be the source of moral wisdom—the idea that existence, deeply and richly enough understood, might somehow yield normative insight.

There would be great danger, however, in transforming these fragments of what might be called "ecological" or "structural" awareness into the philosophical and legal scaffolds of an even braver new world. For the sanctification of nature or of "natural principles," even if achievable and even if effective in actually protecting natural systems,[51] would simply return us to the religious tradition that preceded transcendence, the tradition in which the divine, far from an other-worldly essence, was immanent in all that is. It was the tradition of immanence that was exemplified by the pantheistic belief that all objects and places in the natural world possessed guardian spirits demanding propitiation as security against unspeakable harm.

To restore anything like pagan animism would be to risk sanctifying the present, with all its faults and inadequacies. Treating the existing order as sacred (or, in a secularized version of immanence, as immutable) might well relegate to permanent subjugation and deprivation those many who are not now among the privileged, freezing the social evolution of humanity into its contemporary mold. It would thus be as misguided to act on the premise that plastic trees are "bad" simply because they are "unnatural" as I have argued it would be mistaken to act as though there could be no objection to plastic trees so long as persons have come to like them. Unless evolving human consciousness and will are recognized as legitimate and indeed vital parts of the natural order, there can exist only sterility and paralysis, negating all possibility of critique and progress.

D. A Possible Synthesis

To be free, it seems, is to choose what we shall value. To feel coherence over time and community with others while experiencing freedom is to choose in terms of shared commitments to principles outside ourselves. But to make commitments without destroying freedom is to live by principles that are capable of evolution as we change in the process of pursuing them. If transcendence degenerates ultimately into choice without commitment to principle, and if immanence ultimately disintegrates into principles incapable of change, what must be sought is a synthesis of immanence with transcendence—of sacred observer with grand manipulator.

Such a synthesis requires the sanctification neither of the present nor of progress but of *evolving processes of interaction and change*—processes of action and choice that are valued for themselves, for the conceptions of being that they embody, at the same time that they are valued as means to the progressive evolution of the conceptions, experiences, and ends that characterize the human community in nature at any given point in its history. As those conceptions, experiences, and ends evolve through the processes made possible by a legal and constitutional framework for choice, the framework itself—the society's idealized conception of how change should be structured—may be expected to change as well.

One might think of the evolving framework as a multidimensional spiral along which the society moves by successive stages, according to laws of motion which themselves undergo gradual transformation as the society's position on the spiral, and hence its character, changes. To avoid the spiral's premature closure upon any necessarily tentative set of ideals and expectations, the framework for choice must incorporate procedures for its own evolution. But the framework for choice must begin somewhere, and, like all beginnings, this one will seem, to some, to have come from no place. The only solace must be Wittgenstein's: "Giving grounds [must] come to an end sometime. But the end is not an ungrounded presupposition: It is an ungrounded way of acting."[52]

The framework for choice to which I believe we should initially commit ourselves must have a double aspect. Although it must be selected in light of its likely consequences, it cannot be designed simply to assure that the journey will bring us to some preconceived destination. For no such destination is describable in advance, and in no event could we expect a purely instrumental strategy to liberate us from the grip of instrumentalism and manipulation in which we feel trapped. The "way of acting" to which we commit ourselves must therefore be a process valued in large part for its intrinsic qualities rather than for its likely results alone.

Such a conception of process as more than instrumental should not seem wholly alien. In many realms of human experience, process is intuitively and widely felt to matter in itself. Thus kicking a dog is seen as different from tripping over it; lynching an innocent victim is not thought to be the same as erroneously convicting a person after a fair trial; there are important respects in which the sould of music produced by a computer cannot be equated with the human enterprise of a living orchestra. In the environmental area in particular, given the absence of any final system of ends that either could or should command assent, we should be capable of perceiving intrinsic significance— sanctity, if you will—in the very principles, however variable, according to which we orchestrate our relationships with one another and with the physical world of which we are a part.[53]

But we do not begin wholly without a conception of the distant horizons toward which our processes should grope. Along those horizons, at the very least, one must imagine that change will remain forever possible, and that no single conception or species will perpetually dominate according to an iron rule. Partly because it seems plausible to believe that the processes we embrace must from the beginning prefigure something of that final vision if the vision itself is to be approximated in history, and partly because any other starting point would drastically and arbitrarily limit the directions in which the spiral might evolve, it follows that the processes with which we start should avoid a premise of human domination—or indeed a premise of the total subservience of any form of being to any other.

If the evolving processes we adopt are somehow to synthesize the ideals of immanence with those of transcendence, it follows also that those processes must embody a sense of reverence for whatever stands beyond human wants and their directly willed consequences, as well as a stance of criticism toward all that is given and a commitment to the conscious improvement of the world. Such a synthesis, it should be clear, must eventually cut across the received categories of "nature" and "culture," for implicit in that classic dichotomy is a denial of any possible union between the immanent and the transcendent.

It should not be distressing that this is so, and that traditional conceptions of nature and of the natural will not suffice to capture the necessary objects of our respect and of our sense of obligation. At the most elementary level, after all, the impulse that is felt by many as awe and respect for a vast canyon or a spider's web has much in common with the sense of sanctity felt by others as they stand before the structures at Stonehenge or the Cathedral at Chartres. What differentiates a silent wilderness or a breathtaking monument from a littered campground or a tornado-struck town cannot be summarized in any facile contrast between the works of "man" and those of "nature." To recognize that humanity is a part of nature and the natural order a constituent part of humanity is to acknowledge that something deeper and more complex than the customary polarities must be articulated and experienced if the immanent and transcendent are somehow to be united. At that crossroads, conceptions such as harmony, rootedness in history, connectedness with the future, all seem more pertinent than the ultimately conventional concept of "the natural."

Realizing the synthesis of immanence with transcendence in a conception of process that seeks to overcome the nature-culture dichotomy entails rejecting both simple preservationism or noninterventionism (the two are of course distinct) on the one hand, and manipulative exploitation of the world on the other. The result is consistent with the distinctly western tradition (albeit a distinctly minority tradition in the West) of regarding man as responsible for the perfection of an always incomplete natural order rather than either for its submissive acceptance or for its aggressive conquest.

Such a synthesis provides a fitting contrast both to the primitivist thesis that nature's claims are absolute—that man should do nothing to modify nature (however "nature" is to be defined apart from man) but should be content, at most, to serve as its steward—and to the despotic thesis that man's destiny is to dominate the world, using it however his purposes might dictate. And such a synthesis, finally, offers hope of confronting the paradox that the world beyond man can define his greatness rather than engulfing him in terror only if some dimension of that world remains forever beyond his grasp— that, once the world is seen as man's playground and ultimately his mirror, nothing remains outside himself against which to test his uniqueness or his strength. To give detailed structure and content to this half-way house of process—of *becoming* as the synthesis of accepting and subduing—is a massive task for politics as well as theory. Although it is a task whose precise requirements I am not prepared to describe, at least its beginnings can already be roughly outlined.

III. THE FIRST TURNS OF THE SPIRAL

Like Schiller's mechanics who dare not let the wheels run down while they repair "the living clockwork of the State,"[54] or Neurath's sailors who must rebuild their ship on the open sea without discerning its ideal design,[55] we are condemned to toil in the dimmest light as we feel our way toward the evolution of our conceptions and ideals of the natural order. But if, as we have concluded, the spiral that traces such evolution is to reject human domination over other modes of being, then at least its first turns seem within our grasp. At a minimum, we must begin to extricate our nature-regarding impulses from the conceptually oppressive sphere of human want satisfaction, by encouraging the elaboration of perceived obligations to plant and animal life and to objects of beauty in terms that do not falsify such perceptions from the very beginning by insistent "reference to human interests."[e] Thus environmental impact surveys and statements might make explicit reference to obligations felt toward nature. Resources might be devoted to improving our technical capacity to incorporate such felt obligations in policy analyses. And legislation might be enacted to permit the bringing of claims directly on behalf of natural objects without imposing the requirement that such claims be couched in terms of interference with human use.

A related proposal was recently advanced by Christopher Stone, who suggested the appointment of guardians or trustees for objects in the environment[56] as institutional embodiments of a perceived obligation to treat the world about us with respect, and as symbols of a recognition that persons are not the only entities in the world that can be thought to possess rights. Despite Kant's protest that "man . . . can have no duty to any being other than man,"[57] and despite insistence that, as a matter of "logic," only human beings can have "rights,"[58] the fact is that even our own legal system has long recognized entities other than individual human beings—churches, partnerships, corporations, unions, families, and occasionally even animals—as rightsholders for a wide variety of purposes.

Acceptance of the notion that some previously "rightless" entity enjoys legal protection is largely a matter of acculturation. Arguing for "rights" on behalf of nonhuman entities should be confused neither with proposing that their "wants" should be discerned and then included in the aggregating calculus of choice, nor with suggesting that certain nonhuman interests should have absolute priority over conflicting human claims. Recognizing rights in a previously rightless entity is entirely consistent with acknowledging circumstances in which such rights might be overridden (just as human rights may themselves come into conflict), but it is inconsistent with the unstructured perspective of simply maximizing a homogeneous entity called "total satisfaction."

It remains true that treating a class of entities as rightsholders is compatible with regarding their protected status as a mere juristic

---

[e]John Passmore, "Removing the Rubbish," *Encounter*, April 1974, p. 19. Professor Passmore, it should be said, insists that any ethic elaborating man's relation to land and to the life it sustains *must* be justified by such reference to human interests. The dispute is merely semantic if "human interests" are defined so broadly as to encompass the "interest" in acting altruistically or otherwise fulfilling human obligations; it is anything but semantic if "human interests" are construed to include only the satisfaction of personal preferences.

convention. Thus, although American law has long accepted the independent juridical status of corporations, no one would suggest today that such entities are anything but legal constructs. No law prohibits the death or dismemberment of corporations on the basis of their intrinsic "right to life." No jurisprudence rationalizes the validity of corporate law in terms of "just" propitiation of the endogenous needs of corporate entities. It seems likely that most contemporary observers would view the independent legal status of environmental objects in essentially the same way that they view the concept of corporate existence. Affording legal rights to endangered species and threatened wilderness areas might thus be regarded as a convenient technique for concentrating congeries of otherwise diffuse esthetic and ecological concerns ultimately reducible to individual human interest—in other words, as a useful but quite transparent legal fiction.

Even if this were the most one could hope for, the concept of rights for natural objects would probably represent a valuable doctrinal innovation. Whatever unnecessary threat the "standing" requirement continues to pose to effective environmental action would be avoided. And procedural devices far less cumbersome than class actions would become available for challenging environmental abuses. But we might plausibly hope for more. At least so long as we remain within empathizing distance of the objects whose rights we seek to recognize at any given point in history, it seems reasonable to expect the acknowledgment of such rights to be regarded as more than fictitious. Thus, protecting cats and dogs from torture on the basis of their right to be free from pain and hence our obligation not to mistreat them seems less jarring conceptually today than does protecting a forest from clear-cutting on the theory that the threatened tress have an inherent "right to life."

It is not surprising that one of the few pieces of existing federal law aimed unambiguously at protecting nonhuman interests—the Federal Laboratory Animal Welfare Act—limits its protection to mammals, whose perceptions of pain and discomfort we presume to be similar to our own. In addition to supporting a general hypothesis that the claims of creatures close to man on the evolutionary scale are easier to assimilate into contemporary value systems than are the needs of our more distant relatives, the legislative history of the 1970 amendments to the Act also provides a graphic illustration of the process of anthropomorphic validation. The House committee report proclaims that the purpose of the legislation is to ensure that animals are "accorded the basic *creature comforts* of adequate housing, ample food and water, reasonable handling, *decent sanitation* . . . and adequate veterinary care including the appropriate use of *pain*-killing drugs. . . ."[59]

The statutory terms reveal an obvious transference of human values to the nonhuman rights holders: the words "comfort," "decent sanitation," and indeed "pain" refer to human experiences and perceptions. By incorporating such terms into legislation protecting animals, the draftsmen are equating the perceptions of animals with those of humans; the terminology subliminally reinforces our sympathy for the plight of mistreated animals by evoking images of human suffering. As a result, the propriety of legal protection on behalf of the animals themselves becomes more apparent. As the evolutionary distance between man and nonhuman rights holders increases, the difficulty of analogizing to human experiences mounts. Torturing a dog evokes a strong sympathetic response; dismembering a frog produces a less acute but still unambiguous image of pain; even pulling the wings off a fly may cause a sympathetic twinge; but who would flinch at exterminating a colony of protozoa?

When legal protection is sought for plant life, the obstacles to convincing analogy are greater still. Yet even here the prospects are not altogether hopeless. Humans share certain fundamental needs with plants. Humans and plants both require water, oxygen, and nutrition; both grow and reproduce; both die. Some research even suggests that plants exhibit electrical and chemical reactions functionally analogous to pain.[60] A set of basic reference points for analogizing plant requirements to human needs thus exists. And, once the bases for empathy are established, biologists and ecologists can obviously enrich our understanding of what "needs" exist for the other life forms with whom we have begun to feel new kinship.

What is crucial to recognize is that the human capacity for empathy and identification is not static; the very process of recognizing *rights* in those higher vertebrates with whom we can already empathize could well pave the way for still further extensions as we move upward along the spiral of moral evolution. It is not only the human liberation movements—involving first blacks, then women, and now children—that advance in waves of increased consciousness. The inner dynamic of every assault on domination is an ever broadening realization of reciprocity and identity. Viewed from a slightly different perspective, new possibilities for respect and new grounds for community elevate both master and slave simultaneously, reaffirming the truth that the oppressor is among the first to be liberated when he lifts the yoke, that freedom can be realized only in fidelity to obligation.

A passage in Faulkner's *Absalom, Absalom!* may hold the key: "Maybe happen is never once but like ripples maybe on water after the pebble sinks, the ripples moving on, spreading, the pool attached by a narrow umbilical water-cord to the next pool. . . ."[61] Yet there are some shores too remote for even these concentric circles to reach in the foreseeable future. When it is urged that legal protection be extended to nonliving entities like canyons and cathedrals—not for our sake alone but also for theirs, and not because of what they would "want" but because of our responsibility to them and thus to ourselves—it may be precisely such distant shores at which we are asked to gaze. Saint Francis of Assisi could embrace Brother Fire and Sister Water, but western societies in the last third of this century may be unable to entertain seriously the notion that a mountain or a seashore has intrinsic needs and can make independent moral claims upon our designs.

Still we can try. We can set aside resources and create public authorities for the specific purpose of preserving intact at least some major areas of real wilderness while we convert others into more Walt Disney Worlds and Coney Islands. The very process of treating some places with such respect may itself reveal and even create conceptual possibilities beyond our present capacities. If certain choices do not merely implement but in fact alter the value systems within which they are made, then choosing to accord nature a fraternal rather than an exploited role—even though the argument for so treating nature itself appeals ultimately to human interests, and even when the resulting institutions resolve in particular cases not to forego certain human opportunities "for nature's sake"—might well make us different persons from the manipulators and subjugators we are in danger of becoming.

CONCLUSION

I have described only a possible (I think a plausible) first turn along the spiral of process through which we might grope toward an evolving environmental ethic. I certainly do not claim that I have described an answer. Indeed, the first step has already exposed its own weakness in its obviously indeterminate character (it says very little about how to decide actual cases) and in its inability to deal adequately with the notion that nonliving nature exists for itself—its paradoxical (but seemingly unavoidable) reliance on selfishness to defend the independent value of altruism and on empathy to reveal the independent structure of obligation.

But it is at this juncture that the profound significance of devotion to process should become apparent, for the vision of process I have sought to sketch transcends the intermediate stances of consciousness achieved at discrete points along the spiral's path. Its insistence on the continuing reformulation and evolution of the principles distilled at each stage provides a way not only of bridging the gap between successive stages but also of energizing the journey through a commitment to overcome the inevitable inadequacies at each stage. Thus consciousness remains in a double stance: while vigorously living out the values implicit in our present stage of development, we remain aware of the fact that these values themselves pass through evolutionary stages whose unfolding we participate in and sanctify. All I have said, therefore, has been written rather more in the subjunctive than in the indicative.

Upon that cautionary note, it is appropriate to recall this essay's governing metaphor. The plastic trees of Los Angeles are tangible symbols of a view of nature that coincides with the currently myopic premises of environmental law and policy. The trees represent nature abstracted to pure categories of human interest: they provide shade, decoration, and the esthetic semblance of a natural environment. What's wrong with plastic trees? The question can be answered only tentatively (and there will no doubt be contexts in which the right answer is: "nothing's wrong"), but I have responded, in general, by expressing an ethical impulse toward nature which is irreducible to sophisticated self-interest or even to the question of what the trees "would wish" if they had wishes and could express them. It is an impulse we may well violate when we use "nature surrogates" to conceal the wounds we inflict on the natural order, thereby anesthetizing our aesthetic and ecological sensibilities.

In some circumstances, even the seemingly innocuous act of supplementing the inadequacies of nature with human artifacts—erecting plastic trees where the soil is too poor or shallow or the atmosphere too fouled to support real vegetation—may thus transgress the imperatives of an emerging environmental ethic. Much like black lawn boy statuary that once defaced too many suburban yards, plastic trees implicitly reduce the entities they portray to terms of serviceability, utility and adornment. And such caricatures in turn reinforce the belief that the depicted objects exist not for themselves but only to serve a universe of desires and needs.

What is required, I have argued, is a rejection of this philosophy, itself a legacy of an antiworldly, transcendent conception of the universe, but without a return to the immanent conception in which the natural was worshipped and human consciousness excluded from the vital place I believe it must always occupy. If this essay's necessarily sketchy argument for a synthesis of the immanent with the transcendent has seemed to tilt toward immanence, it has done so largely in reaction to the almost obsessive devotion in our time to a secularized version of the transcendent, in which human will and instrumental reason have become the engine of a pilotless locomotive, hurtling through a terrain devoid of intrinsic value.

Shortly after World War II, Horkheimer asked us to imagine what a purely formal mode of reason in a valueless environment would ultimately mean:

> We cannot maintain that the pleasure a man gets from a landscape . . . would last long if he were convinced *a priori* that the forms and colors he sees are just forms and colors, that all structures in which they play a role are purely subjective and have no relation whatsoever to any meaningful order or totality, that they simply and necessarily express nothing. . . . No walk through the landscape is necessary any longer; and thus the very concept of landscape as experienced by a pedestrian becomes meaningless and arbitrary. Landscape deteriorates altogether into landscaping.[62]

What mind can resist despair at such a prospect? However paradoxical might be the appeal to individual human interest in an argument meant partly to criticize such appeals, who can fail to admit that the logic of self-interest leads finally not to human satisfaction but to the loss of humanity itself?

NOTES

1. David Brower, in *Time and the River Flowing*, by Francois Leydet, ed. by D. Brower (New York: Ballantine Books, 1968), p. 159 (writing of a cavern once called the Cathedral in the Desert, now submerged by Lake Powell).

2. Charles Baudelaire, "Rêve Parisien," in *Flowers of Evil* (New York: New Directions, 1955), p. 103.

3. See *Los Angeles Times*, Feb. 8, 1972, sec. 2, at 6, col. 2.

4. See *Los Angeles Times*, Feb. 22, 1972, sec. 2, at 1, col. 3.

5. Martin H. Krieger, "What's Wrong with Plastic Trees?" *Science* 179 (February 1973): 446, 451.

6. *Ibid.* at 451, 453.

7. Joseph Morgenstern, "What Hath Disney Wrought!" *Newsweek*, October 18, 1971, p. 38.

8. National Environmental Policy Act of 1969, secs. 102 (2) (A), 102 (2) (B), 42 U.S.C. Secs. 4332 (2) (A), 4332 (2) (B) (1970).

9. Cf. Laurence H. Tribe, "Trial by Mathematics: Precision and Ritual in the Legal Process," *Harvard Law Review*, vol. 84 (1971), pp. 1329, 1361-65, 1389-90.

10. See Bruce Ackerman, et al., *The Uncertain Search for Environmental Quality* (New York: The Free Press, 1974), pp. 101–46.

11. Conversation with author, in Santa Monica, Cal., Dec. 7, 1971.

12. See Ralph d'Arge, "Economic Policies, Environmental Problems and Land Use: A Discussion of Some Issues and Strategies in Research," July 25–August 5, 1972, p. 14 (background paper for NSF Conference on Research Needs in Planning Our Physical Environment, Boulder, Colo.).

13. See Peter C. Fishburn, "Lexicographic Orders, Utilities and Decision Rules: A Survey," August 1972 (unpublished).

14. See Laurence H. Tribe, "Policy Science: Analysis or Ideology?" *Philosophy and Public Affairs*, vol. 2 (1972), pp. 88–93. (hereinafter cited as "Policy Science"), in *Benefit-Cost and Policy Analysis 1972, An Aldine Annual on Forecasting, Decision-Making, and Evaluation*, ed. by W. Niskanen, A. Harberger, R. Haveman, R. Turvey & R. Zeckhauser (Chicago: Aldine Publishing Co., 1972), pp. 3–47.

15. *Ibid.* at 87 n. 54, 88–89 and n. 56; *idem.*, "Technology Assessment and the Fourth Discontinuity: The Limits of Instrumental Rationality," *Southern California Law Review* 46 (1973): 629–630 & n. 44 (hereinafter cited as "Technology Assessment").

16. See, e.g., Alice M. Rivlin, *Systematic Thinking for Social Action* (Washington, D.C.: Brookings Institution, 1971), p. 7.

17. See, e.g., Robert Dorfman and Henry D. Jacoby, "A Model of Public Decisions Illustrated by a Water Pollution Policy Problem," in *Public Expenditures and Policy Analysis*, ed. by R. Haveman & J. Margolis (Chicago: Markham Publishing Company, 1970).

18. Aaron Wildavsky, "The Political Economy of Efficiency: Cost-Benefit Analysis, Systems Analysis, and Program Budgeting," *Public Administration Review* 26 (1966): 292, 308.

19. See Tribe, "Policy Science," pp. 99–100; *idem.*, "Technology Assessment," pp. 634–35, 642–50.

20. See National Environmental Policy Act of 1969 (NEPA), secs. 101 (b); 42 U.S.C. secs. 4331 (b) (1970).

21. See Tribe, "Technology Assessment," pp. 652–54. As I sought to show in "Technology Assessment," such reasoned commitments can be shaped only in communities of persons whose shared experiences and understandings facilitate a common groping toward communal ends. See also Robert Nisbet, *The Quest for Community* (London: Oxford University Press, 1953), pp. 229–232, 235–237, 241–247, 264–271, 276–279. This is so in part for contingent reasons—because it seems unlikely in this period of history that the search for ends can generate fruitful and convincing conclusions when pursued by isolated individuals—and in part as a matter of definition, because the wholeness that in fact seems

threatened by freedom in the choice of ends is wholeness among persons (community) as well as wholeness over time (continuity). See Tribe, "Technology Assessment," p. 651 n. 118.

22. Max Horkheimer, *Eclipse of Reason* (New York: The Seabury Press, 1947), p. 5.

23. *Ibid.* at 18.

24. Immanuel Kant, *The Metaphysical Principles of Virtue*, trans. by J. Ellington (New York: Bobbs-Merrill, 1964), secs. 16–17, pp. 105–106 (hereinafter cited as *Principles of Virtue*).

25. See Jeremy Bentham, *An Introduction to the Principles of Morals and Legislation* (Garden City, N.Y.: Doubleday, 1961), Ch. XVII, sec. 1, para. 4, p. 273 n. 330 (hereinafter cited as *Morals and Legislation*).

26. John Rawls, *A Theory of Justice* (Cambridge, Mass: The Belknap Press of Harvard University, 1971), p. 512.

27. *Ibid.*

28. For insight into these twin risks, I am indebted to Elizabeth Anne Socolow (personal letter, dated August 15, 1974).

29. See John Stuart Mill, *Utilitarianism* (Garden City, N.Y.: Doubleday Dolphin ed., 1961), pp. 433–434.

30. *Ibid.* at p. 434.

31. See Wildavsky, "Political Economy," pp. 294, 298.

32. See, e.g., Robert Bellah, "Transcendence in Contemporary Piety," in *Beyond Belief: Essays on Religion in a Post-Traditional World* (New York: Harper and Row, 1970), pp. 196–208.

33. See Lynn White, "The Historical Roots of Our Ecological Crisis," *Science* 155 (March 1967): 1203–1205, in *Machina Ex Deo: Essays in the Dynamism of Western Culture* (Cambridge, Mass.: MIT Press, 1968).

34. Some aspects of this thesis parallel the thought and writing of the Frankfurt School. See, generally, Martin Jay, *The Dialectical Imagination: A History of the Frankfurt School and the Institute of Social Research 1923–1950* (Boston: Little, Brown, 1973).

35. See, e.g., Max Weber, *The Protestant Ethic and the Spirit of Capitalism*, trans. by T. Parsons (New York: Scribner's, 1958), pp. 26–7, 75–8, 155–74.

36. See William Leiss, *The Domination of Nature* (New York: G. Braziller, 1972), pp. 45–71.

37. See Roberto Mangabeira Unger, *Knowledge and Politics* (New York: The Free Press, 1975).

38. David Hume, *A Treatise of Human Nature* (Oxford: The Clarendon Press, 1958), bk. II, pt. 3, sec. iii.

39. Jean Paul Sartre, *Existentialism and Humanism*, trans. by P. Mairet (London: Methuen, 1948).

40. Martin Heidegger, *Uber Den Humanismus* (Frankfurt: V. Klosterman, 1949).

41. Thomas Nagel, "Rawls on Justice," *Philosophy Review*, vol. 82 (1973) pp. 220, 228.

42. John Rawls, *A Theory of Justice*, p. 28.

43. *Ibid.*, pp. 62, 137, 142–144.

44. *Ibid.*, p. 512.

45. Bentham, *Morals and Legislation*, ch. XVII, sec. 1, para. 4, p. 273 in 330.

46. Mark Sagoff, "On Preserving the Natural Environment," *Yale Law Journal* 84 (1974): 205, 222. See reply by Laurence Tribe, "From Environmental Foundations to Constitutional Structures: Learning from Nature's Future," *Yale Law Journal* 84 (1975): 545.

47. See Horkheimer, *Eclipse of Reason*, Ch. 1.

48. Christopher D. Stone, "Should Trees Have Standing?—Toward Legal Rights for Natural Objects," *Southern California Law Review* 45 (1972): 490 (hereinafter cited as "Should Trees Have Standing?").

49. Edward Shils, "The Sanctity of Life," *Encounter*, January 1967, pp. 39, 41, 42.

50. See, e.g., Howard Earl Gardner, *The Quest for Mind: Piaget, Lévi-Strauss, and the Structural Movement* (New York, Knopf, 1972).

51. For an argument that "the belief that nature is sacred can tell against attempts to preserve it," see John Passmore, *Man's Responsibility for Nature: Ecological Problems and Western Traditions* (New York: Scribner's, 1974), pp. 173–195.

52. Ludwig Wittgenstein, *On Certainty*, ed. by G.E.M. Anscombe and G. H. von Wright (New York: Harper and Row, 1969), Sec. 110.

53. This attribution of intrinsic significance to process cannot be achieved simply by injecting procedural variables into instrumental analyses. Apart from the complex circularity inherent in the fact that any analysis must become part of the process it has helped to shape, see Tribe, "Policy Science," p. 83, idem.; "Technology Assessment," p. 633 n. 54, any such strategy wrongly assumes that change can be achieved by thought alone and simultaneously forgets that process must remain in part the end and not simply the means.

54. Friedrich Schiller, *On the Aesthetic Education of Man*, trans. by R. Snell (New York: Frederick Ungar, 1965), p. 29.

55. Neurath, "Protokollsatze," *Erkenntnis*, vol. 3 (1932), pp. 204, 206.

56. See Stone, "Should Trees Have Standing?"

57. Kant, *Principles of Virtue*, sec. 16, p. 105.

58. Passmore, "Removing the Rubbish," p. 19.

59. H.R. Rep. No. 1651, 91st Cong., 2d sess. 2(1970) (emphasis added). For the 1970 amendments themselves, see Act of Dec. 24, 1970, pub. L. No. 91-579, 84 Stat. 1560.

60. See, e.g., Cleve Backster, "Evidence of a Primary Perception in Plant Life," *International Journal of Parapsychology*, vol. 10 (1968), p. 329.

61. William Faulkner, *Absalom, Absalom!* (New York: Random House, Vintage ed., 1972), p. 261.

62. Horkheimer, *Eclipse of Reason*, pp. 37–38.

✳ Chapter Four

The Rights of Nature

Charles Frankel

A good deal of the concern over environmental
protection stems from the feeling that something known as
"Nature" has rights or needs, and that industrial society is
careless of these. What is it people have in mind when they say this?
How can Nature, which is not in any obvious sense a moral agent or a
unified, sentient thing, have any rights? What would our social
planning be like if we set about to take care of "the rights of Nature"
in some systematic way? And, to go one step farther back, is a
secular, "homocentric" approach to morals and values capable of
articulating or defending the principles on which a theory of "the
rights of Nature" depends? What follows is a first effort on my part
to sort out my thoughts on these matters. Happily, one starts with
the help of a considerable deposit of thought in the western
tradition.

I. "NATURE" IN SMALL CASE

The use of the word "Nature" in capitalized form is continuous with,
but nevertheless different from, the use of the word in an
uncapitalized form, as when we speak of "the nature of mules" or
"the nature of war." In this latter use, the word refers, usually, to
salient features of a class of things or events, selected because, with
the help of appropriate generalizations, they allow us to explain or
predict other significant characteristics of the things or events in
question. Thus, it is the "nature" of water to boil at 100°C., and it is
the "nature" of man to live in groups.

Sometimes, to be sure, the word "nature" is used to characterize
not the significant traits of a class but those of an individual. We
speak, for example, of "Hamlet's nature" or of the peculiar "nature"

of a particular chess game. In such cases, even though we are describing and explaining an individual thing, person, or event, we are still doing so with the use of generalizations. Classification remains implicit in the process. A "nature" is a system of regularities. Thus an explanation of Hamlet's behavior in terms of his "nature" might refer to his scrupulousness about condemning people on insufficient evidence, and his incapacity to act without watching and commenting on himself. These traits, in general, are known to accompany other traits, such as the tendency to delay action, to miss opportunities, and to move in a crooked path towards one's goal. They are thus organizing traits, which help us to understand a broad spectrum of Hamlet's behavior: they constitute his individual "nature."

The term "nature" when used in this way is an instrument that helps us to draw inferences and make predictions. It derives its use from the presupposition that there are certain general laws on the basis of which we are justified in saying, "If A then B." The term "nature" so used is not the name of anything. Fire has a nature, and Hamlet has a nature, but this is no more than to say that fire has the property of intense heat, or that Hamlet has the property of being thoughtful, and that from these traits we can deduce other important things about fire or Hamlet. A thing's "nature" is not a motor or a ghost inside it; it is merely that thing's traits, or rather some of them, organized in a logically coherent way. But implicit in the conception that things have "natures" is the idea that there is something hard and resistant about them; that they follow laws and can only be changed in accordance with laws; that their structure is independent, at least in part, of what we will, so that we must pay a price when we deal with them. We cannot follow every random impulse but must find the right key and adopt a correct method.

II. THE RELATIVITY OF "NATURE"

A thing's "nature" may be variously defined, depending on the purpose at hand. It is the "nature" of pigs to be dirty; it is also the "nature" of pigs to be delicious when properly cooked. The neglect of the evident point that definitions of a thing's or a class's "nature" are relative to specific purposes is responsible for the recurrent fallacy of assuming that, because it is the "nature" of a species or an individual to be X, it cannot be, or should not be, converted to Y. It is the "nature" of elephants to be wild; they survive and prosper without human intervention and training. But they can be tamed, and there are definite conditions under which this can be said to be the right thing to do. Similarly, the sexual drives of human beings, though inherent in their natures, are nevertheless compatible with complete asceticism. Further, the question of the morality of asceticism cannot be decided by an appeal to "human nature." It requires a prior determination whether that nature is good or corrupt, and whether the suppression of "the natural" serves a necessary or desirable higher purpose.

These remarks do not vitiate the point made earlier, however, to the effect that "nature" contains the notion of something independent of human desires. Though the "nature" of redwood can be defined in a number of ways, depending on whether we are building a greenhouse bench, measuring fire hazards, or considering the costs of creating new redwood forests, there are some characterizations of the "nature" of redwood that are incorrect in any of these contexts, and some characterizations that are more comprehensively useful than others. Usually, these more comprehensive characterizations are provided by the generalizing sciences. It is in this sense, I believe, that we can understand the classic description of the sciences as disciplines that seek "the true nature" of things.

Of course, even in this context the term "nature" retains its relation to a distinct purpose. The object of scientific inquiry is to discover "patterns of relations . . . that are pervasive in vast ranges of fact,"[1] but this object is also the purpose of theologians, philosophers, and poets of the cosmos such as Dante or Goethe. What distinguishes *scientific* characterizations of "the nature of things" is that they are made subject to the regulative principle that inquiry yield results susceptible to experimental verification, and to the further principle that the preferred results are those that generate fruitful new lines of inquiry. Thus the concept of "nature," even in the sciences, carries the mark of a goal seeking animal.

However, the fact that a given theory of the nature of matter—e.g., quantum theory—successfully generates fruitful lines of further inquiry is not a fact simply about the structure of tastes of the human mind or the objectives of inquiry in a given culture. A theory's fruitfulness also tells us something about independent characteristics of the world. To deny this, so far as I can see, is ultimately to deny that the data of experience have any content independent of the conceptual categories into which we fit them. No doubt, depending on conceptual categories, a pain behind the eyes can be read as the visitation of a spirit, as eyestrain, or as the sign of a suppressed desire to quit work.

But is the datum itself—the feeling of pain—entirely concept dependent? It seems doubtful that we cannot even experience pain except in the framework of a specific idea or interpretation of pain; it seems equally doubtful that the toothaches of Hopi Indians and Parisian existentialists are entirely incomparable experiences. Pain, the gold in a sunset, the halo around a star, are there to be observed whatever the culture, era, or conceptual paradigm. It is true that percepts without concepts are blind, just as concepts without percepts are empty. But percepts, if I am right, also have an irrepressible independence about them—a variability from the rule, an unpredictability in some element or other to which the concepts at hand have given no clue. It is this character in our percepts, I believe, that assures us that there is something in existence besides our ideas, something richer than the conceptual maps by which we make our way.

This epistemological reflection, sketchy though it is, may seem a lengthy digression. But it is central, I think, to discussions of "the rights of Nature," to say nothing of the view that modern scientific ideas of "Nature" are somehow expressive of or conducive to callousness about the physical environment. We shall come to the direct discussion of these matters, but at this preliminary stage it is useful to clear the deck by reminding ourselves of the currents of philosophical opinion which have received considerable recent attention, and which seem on the way to sociologizing quite completely the concept of "nature."[a] Though I must state the point so briefly as to risk dogmatism, it appears to me that to erase from science the concept of "nature," standing for something independent of human perspective, is to remove the lynchpin from the system of principles that direct scientific inquiry, and that distinguish it from other forms of human communication and cooperation.

Because scientific theories satisfy human purposes that are historically determined, it does not automatically follow that they do not also reveal something about the independent, unhistorical constitution of things. The concept of nature entertained by the sciences at any time is not a product of sociological structures and functions alone, any more than the shape and weight of a saw is explicable only in terms of the special history and needs of carpentering in a given culture. The characteristics of wood have something to do with the matter as well, which explains why saws tend to have certain constant characteristics of their own no matter where you see them. In sum, although it is true that the particular order that physics here and now makes of the world is connected to

[a]The work of Thomas Kuhn, and, in a more extreme form, Paul Feyerabend, illustrates this tendency.

the historic purposes of physicists, and is shaped by the contingencies of time and place, this is not at all the same thing as to say that one era's "nature" is inevitably another era's "ideology."

III. "NATURE": ONE OR MANY?

The notion of "nature" as designating those traits of the world that permit the most comprehensive ordering and explaining of phenomena, subject to the demands for continuing inquiry, is compatible, it should be noted, with a pluralistic as well as monistic conception of the universe. George Washington's soldierly character was independent of his bad teeth; the fact that Kennedy's assassin succeeded while Hitler's didn't is independent of the characters of Kennedy or Hitler. Individual events or things are bundles of contingency: they possess combinations of traits that cannot all be brought together into a single logically related system. Moreover, to put this down to our present level of ignorance, and to suppose that an omniscient observer would be bound to see every aspect of every individual thing as necessarily related to everything else, is to suppose that an omniscient observer would regard all distinctions between things and all temporal and partial discourse about them as illusory. Whatever may be said for such a supposition, it would leave us still requiring a system of contingencies to make our way through our illusory world.

There exists, in any case, no single science—e.g., physics—into which the explanation of all phenomena can be compressed. To be sure, nothing that exists is exempt from the laws of physics. But this does not imply that every aspect of everything—e.g., the plans in our minds, the characteristics of the American Constitution, the sorrows of young Werther—can be characterized or explained in physicists' terms. Accordingly, to be a determinist is not to rule out chance from the workings of the universe. So far as our existing knowledge goes, nature as a whole isn't a whole. It is a miscellany. The grammatical fact that we use the singular "it" to refer to it should not mislead us about what we have the intellectual right to say about it.

The idea of the unity of nature nevertheless persists. It has its origins in the monotheistic heritage of our civilization, and in the Greek philosophers' efforts to rationalize their polytheistic religious tradition. But it survives because it serves an indispensable intellectual function, particularly in science where it exercises its power as a unifying *ideal*—a goal by which inquiry is steered even though reaching that goal is not possible. "Nature," as used in scientific language—Nature with an implied capital letter—names the ideal object of the scientific purpose. It represents the hope of achieving inclusive generalizations.

IV. "NATURE" CAPITALIZED

"Nature," so conceived, is to be contrasted most sharply with the Supernatural. What characterizes the Supernatural is the power to make exceptions, to pass miracles, to upset the senseless routines of the world, to play deliberate favorites. In contrast, if the success of modern science teaches anything, it teaches that the most reliable comprehensive generalizations are those that explain events in terms remote from the categories of human desire. Prayers, bets, willing, revenge, justice, mercy, have no efficacy in Nature's order. Even in the field of human behavior, where human desires have causal efficacy, the tendency of social scientific intelligence is to emphasize the unintended and undesired consequences of these desires, and the far greater causal efficacy of biological and institutional structures which have characteristics independent of the human will. The scientific use of the term "Nature" is an antidote to thoughts of human omnipotence. One of the myths propagated by the defenders of supernaturalism is that those in the tradition of Lucretius deny the limitations of man.

Behind this myth, however, there is sometimes a nagging and not easily put down question that has every air of plausibility. "Nature" as the ideal object of the scientific purpose is without an encompassing moral design. Any "value" found in it is found by taking some partial and limited point of view, by asking how nature affects some organized natural entity possessing an inner *conatus*. Thus it is that "Nature" comes to be seen, the dissatisfied questioner then points out, "solely in terms of potential human satisfaction."[2] And in the end this is to destroy the satisfaction human beings draw from it. In Max Horkheimer's words, "We cannot maintain that the pleasure a man gets from a landscape . . . would last long if he were convinced *a priori* that the forms and colors he sees are just forms and colors, that all structures in which they play a role are purely subjective and have no relation whatsoever to any meaningful order or totality. . . . Landscape deteriorates altogether into landscaping."[3] And so a culture dominated by such a concept of Nature ends, it is said, by being unable to say why plastic trees aren't as good as real trees if only they serve human interests as satisfactorily.

But why would plastic trees *not* be as good as real trees if they served human interests equally well? Indeed, suppose real trees in a certain region turned out to be nesting places for insects carrying a deadly sleeping sickness, and the only specific effective against the insects also killed the trees and ruined the soil. Would not plastic trees be better than real trees in this context? And would people's religions or metaphysical beliefs make any difference in reaching such a judgment, provided they included no specific taboos against killing insects or relieving human suffering and no conception of a cosmic plan that forbade intervention in natural processes? After our nineteenth and twentieth century experiences with the restrictive idea of a "Natural Law" in relation to efforts to alter economic relations, it seems almost majestically imprudent to revive, in scarcely disguised form, the notion that there are lines human beings should never cross, no matter what the exigent circumstance.

The fact is that, in the hypothetical circumstances described, most people, whether they called themselves "immanentist," "transcendentalist," or "positivist," would opt for plastic trees, and would do so on grounds of the human interests served. And most people do not normally opt for plastic trees for the very simple and direct reason that, in normal circumstances, plastic trees are lamentably inadequate substitutes for real trees as servants of human interests. Plastic trees don't smell like real trees, don't secrete moisture, don't turn toward the sun, don't look fresh in the morning, don't whisper mysteriously at night, don't have an independent life of their own. These are all precious values in human experience.

In brief, a fundamental fallacy in the idea that a scientific view of "Nature" leads inexorably to the worship of plastic man in a plastic landscape is that it confuses a *theory about values* (e.g., a value is that which serves a human interest) with *the values themselves*. What people think about plastic trees as substitutes for real trees depends on the *content* of their preferences and not on whether they also make those preferences the preferences of the universe as a whole. An outlook such as Spinoza's or Bertrand Russell's, which denies the executive order of things has a moral design, is perfectly compatible with love for the beauties and irreplaceable vitalities of natural things.

Similarly, a philosophical utilitarian need not be a man who thinks that nothing is of value that bakes no bread. It was hard-headed Bentham who thought it quite enough as an argument for kindness to animals to remind us that animals suffer. In counting human interests we must count human powers of empathy, and there is no evidence that appeals to compassion for animals have been less effective in protecting them than appeals to theologico-metaphysical beliefs asserting that cruelty violates an antecedent moral law. On the contrary, the historical evidence suggests that it has been in the countries where "science" and "utility" have been most popular that the humane treatment of animals and the deliberate concern to protect natural things have flourished most.

We must also distinguish between the "homocentric" view that "human interests" are the measures of all value and the "individualist" view that treats "individual human need and desire as the ultimate frame of reference."[4] A frequent tendency is to confuse the two. But while Aristotle, for example, was "homocentric"—that is to say, he was a eudaemonist who judged values in relation to the supreme goal of human happiness—Aristotle was not "individualistic." He recognized the *polis* as the seat of values greater—more conducive to the attainment of ideal happiness—than any that individuals by themselves might conceive, seek, or find. The recognition of collective goods, and of schemes of obligation whose rationale lies in their necessity for the survival and prosperity of human enterprises transcending the generations, is in fact a common, even if not universal, feature of "homocentric" ethics from Aristotle through Spinoza to John Dewey.

Nor is this an illogical inference for philosophers in this tradition to have drawn. "Human interests" are what they are, and many human interests are not self-centered or individually oriented: people sacrifice themselves for their children, they demand justice, they hunt for the Holy Grail. To argue that because all values are human values, all values reduce to "the satisfaction of individual human wants"[5] is a version of the classic egoistic fallacy that asserts that because an altruist in serving others satisfies himself, he is no different from a self-centered man. The difference remains between the kind of thing that satisfies the altruist and that which satisfies the egoist. "Homocentricism," "humanism," "secularism" are not the names of uniquely identifiable substantive schemes of values.

V. "NATURE" IN SCIENCE, HUMANISTIC STUDIES, AND TECHNOLOGY

"Nature" as an object of scientific study is to be contrasted not only with the supernatural but also with human art and creation. The natural is the opposite of the artificial, of what is conceived, willed, made by man. To be sure, within a scientific perspective, art and artifice fall among the natural processes. As I have already suggested, "Nature," as it figures in scientific investigation, is the name of an ideal object—what would be revealed if all inquiries were complete, and all explanations could be given in terms of a single system of comprehensive laws. It is incompatible with such a goal to make the classic categorical distinctions that have been made (and that so many continue to speak of renewing) between "body" and "mind," "nature" and "spirit," "science" and "philosophy." Accordingly, science studies human behavior and accomplishments, but its triumph is to show how these phenomena are events in the larger system of Nature—to explain them as events within a system of relations, such as economic, psychological, or sociological laws, that are not themselves products of human contrivance but are the conditions of such contrivance.

In contrast with the scientific outlook, "humanistic" study tends to put the human mind and ego in the foreground, and to take the measure of "Nature" in terms of its impact on human thought, feeling, well-being, and use. This is true even—indeed, especially—for nature lovers like Thoreau. The woods and fields are important for what they mean to a human soul; they are companions, felt beings with which one lives in closer harmony than with most of one's human fellows. And for the humanist what bulks largest in the scientific conception of "Nature" is the human activity that explains the conception, the work of the mind and imagination in the creation and elaboration of concepts, and in the disciplining of argument and observation.

Nevertheless, "humanistic" study need not be inconsistent with the scientific approach, and a considerable number of the greatest observers of human affairs have combined the two. Sophocles, Thucydides, Shakespeare, Tolstoy, all have stressed, on the one side, the extraordinary fertility and audacity of the human mind and will, their capacity to outrun the predictions and to exist at levels of monstrosity or sublimity that seem to bend nature out of shape. But on the other side they have revealed human beings as inevitably caught in a net of relations and natural laws that carry them, by inexorable force, to a destiny that is not theirs to will. Human beings are like actors on a stage who play their parts perfectly but only come to understand very late, if at all, the full meaning of what they are saying and doing.

It is almost certainly misleading to speak of "the humanist approach" for humanists are various. And it is a gross canard (defined as "an extravagant or absurd report or story set afloat to delude the public")[6] to set "science" against "the humanities" and to suggest that there is something fundamentally incompatible between them. A philosopher or dramatist may see in the human creature's setting himself against Nature, in his distinguishing himself from what is not human and in his proclamation that he is the lord of creation or at least the special trustee of God, the most important thing about man—the source of his nobility, wickedness, pride, and fall. But he may at the same time hold a view like Homer's that individual men and women are like things in the wind, carried by forces they do not control:

> As is the generation of leaves, so is that of humanity. The wind scatters the leaves on the ground, but the live timber burgeons with leaves again in the season of spring returning. So one generation of men will grow while another dies.[7]

There is, in fact, a more clean-cut distinction between the scientific conception of "Nature" and the technological-industrial conception than there is between the outlooks on man and nature of, say, Spinoza, the scientifically oriented philosopher, and Sophocles, the poet and dramatist. What science progressively reveals is the existence of facts and relationships that are what they are whether human beings approve or not, and that exact their inexorable cost no matter what mode of adjustment to them human beings work out. That discovery is one Sophocles' tragic heroes make as well. "Nature," in this sense, is the name of an order or structure unshakeable in its most fundamental characteristics. It imposes limits on human choice; individuals and societies seeking to live well by rational plan and not by happy accident learn as a first lesson that living well, within Nature, means learning a discipline or regimen. This is Spinoza's idea of "Nature," and it is a conception, it should be noted, that calls for classic religious attitudes of acceptance, obedience, and adoration, and not for kicking over the traces.

What leads to a confusion between the scientific and the technological-industrial conceptions of "Nature" is probably that both run afoul of traditional pieties. Scientific explanations of natural phenomena frequently conflict with religious explanations; technology, in parallel fashion, invades territory guarded by sacred precepts and takes it over (as, for example, with the birth control pill). And since technological achievements often also represent the application of scientific knowledge, it is easy to fall into the platitude that a common attitude towards Nature permeates both science and technology. But this is not true. Science and technology have some enemies in common, and they have attitudes towards Nature that have some common elements, but there are also significant differences. The technologist is interested in the appropriation, practical manipulation and exploitation of natural phenomena and relationships; the scientist is concerned with understanding. For the technologist, Nature is raw material; for the scientist it is an object of wonder. For the technologist it is something to be challenged, improved, subdued; for the scientist it is what always triumphs over man, what controls the terms of human existence. (Obviously, I deal with ideal types here. Specific individuals may veer from one attitude to another; and people often hold both attitudes together.)

The distinction is important in understanding one impulse behind statements to the effect that "Nature has rights." The term "rights" is awkward and polyguous at best; to speak of impersonal things such as Nature as having "rights" seems still further to confuse matters. Nevertheless, such a way of speaking—which does, after all, have the stamp of established usage to support it—may be a way of saying, elliptically, that the individuals composing a society have, or should have, a right to the scientific examination of the costs and consequences of using nature for this or that human purpose. Technology deploys means, devices, strategies; but ends, purposes, goals ought also to be examined, for they too are natural events, and Nature never bends to a human purpose without charging a price. In other words, in the context of the distinction between the "scientific" and the "technological" conceptions of "Nature," the expression "Nature has rights" may be said to articulate the claim that the social introduction and use of technology should be subjected to methods of rational appraisal, and that unintended costs and consequences should be sought out.

VI. "NATURE" THE VITAL

"Nature," when defined in terms of the ideals of science, and in contrast to the supernatural, is characterized by traits like impersonality, regularity, predictability, indifference to human feelings. But "Nature" may also be contrasted with the technological, the deliberately planned. So perceived, "Nature" becomes the name of the fertile, the unpredictable, the vital and mysterious.

"Technology" is more than machinery; it is a style, a mode of approaching and perceiving things, a way of organizing them. The most conspicuous feature of this style, probably, is its explicitness. Everything of significance, technologically speaking, can be put into words or abstract symbols. But human experience, whether it is on the human or the nonhuman scene, has implications as well as explications. It is suffused with portents, memories, possibilities, tones, that are not susceptible to being caught in the net of exact language.

> "Tyger, tyger, burning bright
> In the forests of the night."

"Nature"—particularly the Nature of the Romantics—is used as the name for those aspects of experience that overflow the categories of the technologists, that deny "Newton's single vision."

It is in this context, I think, that we should place "Nature" as a name of love for the hills and streams, the forests and animals. These are what have not been turned into human constructs. They make visible a power "far more deeply interfused," not captured or capturable by human wit or will. Reflection will suggest that, in fact, the hills and streams, forests and animals loved by nature poets and others have usually had the benefit of considerable human intervention. They are not trackless jungles, but *preserves;* not scorpions and fever-carrying ticks, but responsive animals who have given their names to human traits ("lion-hearted," "eagle-eyed," "foxy," "dovish") and with whom we have a kind of implied social contract, a communal arrangement of mutual respect. They are *man's* surroundings, relatively tamed; if there is risk in them, the risk is just enough to add pleasurable excitement to life; it is not so large as to make life grim or desperate.

The "wilderness" of the preservationist is not wildness: it is a refuge from technology and cities. Members of civilized societies desire it and value it. They look to it as one corrective to technological explicitness—as an opportunity for the exercise of other powers of body, mind, and intuition than those ordinarily demanded of them. "The rights of Nature" in this meaning may be said to express the claim that there is an indispensable social value in the maintenance of opportunities for such kinds of physical and emotional exercise. The case for these rights, so interpreted, is that a society whose members have no direct experience of Nature will have a joyless conception of the human condition and may well die of technological hubris.

VII. "NATURE" AS A PRINCIPLE OF DEVELOPMENT

The use of "Nature" in which the word stands for the unplanned and untracked, for the vital and the ineffable, comes close to another use of the term in which it is associated with the biological. Physics, in this convention, studies mere "matter"—undeveloping, static in its properties. Biology, in contrast, studies life process—unfolding, growth, decay. And the collection of the laws which govern the stages of unfolding, growth and decay are denominated "Nature."

In the modern world Rousseau is probably the key figure in developing this concept of "Nature." For all his undoubted originality, Rousseau revived an older tradition with regard to appeals to "Nature." Like some of the Greek sophists, he was a spokesman for "Nature" as the green spaces outside the cities, and for the superiority of the moral life in such settings. When men forsook artifice and costumes, so the theory went, they were simple and direct, functional in speech and dress and approach to life; and they were equal in their relation to one another, recognizing the common human purpose of living together and forsaking the cumbersome, unnatural system of inequality, trickery, and rivalry that too much civilization—cityfication—creates. In effect, "Nature" was the name for a process of civilizing mankind—up to a point. "Nature" was not the raw and undeveloped; neither was it the overripe and overdeveloped. It was a word calling on men to remember their origins and not to push their powers of artificial reason and governance too far.

Rousseau's "Nature" of the reasonable peasant was in fact part of a larger conception of "Nature" as a set of principles of development. Man, as a creature of Nature, as a vital and growing being, should be recognized as possessing a distinctive arc of growth. Not that every individual *had* to move through this arc. An individual's desires for affection, for example, though implanted in him by Nature, could be ignored or repressed, so that he grew up incapable of giving love or receiving it. But such an individual would be unhappy, and very probably useless or even dangerous to his fellows. He would be warped, misshaped, like a tree deprived of the sunlight except on one side. "Nature," so used, is the point of departure for most current educational theory and notions of child rearing. And it is not without significance for conceptions of environmental planning: that the human environment should be planned in relation to the needs and idiosyncrasies of the human organism, and that dire consequences flow when it is not, is surely part of what is meant when people object to the destruction of open areas as "violations of Nature."

John Stuart Mill, not himself a product of an education shaped to a child's normal pattern of growth, wrote: "Human nature is not a machine to be built after a model, and set to do exactly the work prescribed for it, but a tree, which requires to grown and develop itself on all sides, according to the tendency of the inward forces which make it a living thing."[8] Rousseau, the product of a Calvinist-Genevan childhood, meant, similarly, to suggest that, in the education of children, their individual needs and the quality of their unfolding intellectual and emotional powers be taken into account. Like educational reformers—e.g., Rabelais—before him, and like Mill, John Dewey, or Bertrand Russell after him, Rousseau's appeal to the "nature" of children was an appeal against pedantry and the imposition of mind-killing disciplines. This concept of "nature" is easily sentimentalized, as Rousseau himself gave proof. Nevertheless, it is not to be automatically confused with the idea that rules as such are bad. Rousseau's appeal to "Nature" hardly made him an apostle of "permissiveness." If a child repeatedly broke windows, he wrote *Emile*, for example, the child should be locked in a windowless room. He would then learn, not by arbitrary punishment but "naturally," by being made to experience the meaning of his actions—why windows were valuable and should not be broken.

The appeal to "Nature," in this tradition, is essentially an effort to correct or reduce arbitrariness, willfulness, and authoritarianism in social relations. The message is that "reason"—the "reason" inherent in adjusting individual behavior and social institutions to the requirements imposed by Nature—ought to be substituted as fully as possible. To this tradition Rousseau added the ingredient of affection. He conceived the desirable kind of social authority as resting on affection and rational conviction rather than on fear, money, superstition, or a tyrant's force of will. Whatever one may think of the practical possibility of achieving such an ideal, it is best understood not as a revolt against classic notions of "Nature" and "Reason" but as an attempt to revive them. It is an exercise in nostalgia, a harking back to the doctrine of Natural Law, and to the effort to show that law rests, ultimately, not on arbitrary will but on reason addressed to the common good. Rousseau greatly altered this tradition precisely because, like Luther or Jonathan Edwards, he was a Revivalist. He wished to inject fresh feeling into it, new moral energy; inevitably, he purified—simplified—the tradition he wished to restore.

In some considerable measure, current appeals to "the rights of Nature" represent this special amalgam of belief and moral attitude: "Nature" is perceived as a system of growth, an order or harmony not to be broken on pain of endangering human happiness and fulfillment. Excessive civilization—too many laws, rules, bureaucrats, schools, computers, too much professionalism, specialization, urbanism, impersonality—is inherently "alienating"; it separates the self from its essential "nature," its inherent tendency of growth. What is needed to repair the world is directness of feeling, simplicity of language and manner, and the warmth of small groups joined by bonds of affection and shared experience.

The tradition for this kind of thinking runs, in this country, from Rousseau through Jefferson and Emerson. Elements of it can be found in Charles Peirce, William James, and John Dewey. It is easy to parody; indeed, the tradition has often engaged in self-parody. Yet it is important to remember the spine of invulnerable good sense that holds it together. It equates "Nature" with the idea of limits to human plasticity. It tells us that there is something under the human skin with its own vitality, something not wholly malleable, not susceptible to Skinnerian conditioning except at the price of destroying spontaneity, talent, zest, vitality.

The values to which people in this tradition appeal may, if one wishes, be called "fragile" values. But they are the durable values celebrated in legend and literature by Panurge, Puck, Scapin, the Marx Brothers, the serpent—the unpredictable idiosyncrasy that breaks the plans, the marvelous waywardness and prolixity of natural forces outrunning man's powers of artifice. The appeal to Nature so construed may be taken as a warning that no social plans, no matter how ingeniously or carefully devised, can annul the random and unpredictable, that it is the inner vitality of human beings that counts for most, and that society should provide the environment likely to safeguard this vitality.

VIII. "NATURE" AS THE PRIMITIVE

As I have suggested, this notion of "Nature" lends itself to grotesque exaggeration. Beginning as a critique of authoritarianism, it becomes, when torn out of context, an appeal to "Nature" against "Culture" in general: a praising of the instinctual, the untutored, the unordered, unhierarchical, unauthorized.

The appeal to "Nature," so understood, becomes an appeal to a disguised principle of Providence. It rests on the assumption that men's fundamental drives are mutually supportive, and that a radical clash between different wills is therefore not possible in "Nature." Only "society" creates such conflicts. Not surprisingly, most of those who hold this view also tend to take it for granted that the "natural" curve of human growth is in the direction of the ethical attitudes they admire. Although they stress the individuality of each person and the glories of diversity and pluralism, they assume that unthwarted, unwarped, truly "individual" and fulfilled people will all be humanitarians, liberals, nature lovers, radicals—whatever they themselves happen to be. Biology and social virtue coincide, as do biology and historical progress—something that Freud never supposed. It is this theologized, or Hegelianized, biology that triumphs (to take examples of two influential books) in Adorno's *Authoritarian Personality* and Marcuse's *Eros in History*.

Hobbes, too, used the term Nature to designate the precivil condition of man. But Hobbes, less impressed by the benevolence of the Creation, took it for granted that this natural state was one to be escaped. If one wishes to be generous, "Naturists" may perhaps be taken as accusers of "society" for bringing out the fierceness in man. Their appeal to "Nature" may be interpreted as a call to review social institutions to take account of the degree to which they do the opposite of what they say—making people more warlike rather than more peaceful, more distrustful rather than trustful. But the act of faith implicit in this appeal to Nature Primitive still bulks large. It is an act of faith bespeaking the life of comfortable people who have had a protected relationship with raw nature, and who live off the fruits of man's thinking and active artisanry while refusing to give these the respect they deserve as expressions of man's nature. The apostles of Nature show a fear of tinkering with nature, of upsetting the delicate harmony of things, that is rarely a fear fixed on anything specific. It indicates in the main the hold of that ancient taboo against eating from the tree of knowledge.

IX. "NATURE" AS A SYSTEM OF SYMBOLS

As may have already been suggested, appeals to "the rights of Nature," like appeals to "property rights," are ways of saying that human beings should have claims over one another's behavior, or, looked at from the opposite end, certain obligations towards one another, with respect towards nonhuman things. They are calls for certain kinds of human conduct.

What kinds of conduct? The answer lies in meanings of the word "Nature" such as those I have attempted to adduce in the preceding pages. The word "Nature" and the associations attached to it symbolize at once the idea of a unified rational system and of biological fertility and unexpectedness; of raw material for human use and of a resistant, implastic power that strikes back when misused; of a primitive origin which it is mankind's pride to have overcome and of a principle of development by which mankind should abide as a condition for its goodness and happiness. Nature's powers, said John Stuart Mill, "are often toward man in the position of enemies, from whom he must wrest, by force and ingenuity, what little he can for his own use. . . . Killing, the most criminal act recognized by human laws, nature does once to every being that lives. . . ."[9]

But Ralph Waldo Emerson, in contrast, wrote in his essay on the same theme that "in the woods we return to reason and faith. There I feel that nothing can befall me in life—no disgrace, no calamity . . . which nature cannot repair. . . ."[10] The word, indeed, is so pregnant with meanings, so full of implications pointing in different directions, that it is not surprising that very large numbers of people should be concerned to defend the rights associated with what it designates. It has something of the flavor of religious words as used by those of a genial Anglican persuasion who do not care much about finer doctrinal points, or doctrinal points at all, but who enjoy feelings of awe and rededication to principle.

Moreover, it is not only the abstract concept of "Nature" that is rich with symbolism. The natural world, in its specifics, is richer still. There in the sky as we see them, sunrise and sunset are for very few of us merely moments in the whirling of the globe. They are signs in the heavens, images of endings and beginnings, pictures of our destiny. We worry about the fate of birds affected by breaches in the aquatic food chain. Is the only reason for our worry the fear of upsetting the "harmony" of natural systems? Or is it also, and probably even more, that eagles, ospreys, and falcons—and whales, sharks, and the little fishes—have a long history as symbols in poetry and religion? Lions, lambs, serpents, doves, mountains, valleys, primroses, thorns, all are wrapped in meanings that give our relation to them its intensity and mystery, and make their destruction or violation portents of the world's impoverishment. It is *this* world of "Nature"—and not only the biologist's or ecologist's—that we want to save when we speak of "the rights of Nature." We want to save a world created by the human imagination, but created in large part "naturally," involuntarily, and coming uncalled back into our imaginations, with the force of natural events, whether we will it or not.

Is it this world that Dr. Horkheimer claims is destroyed when we learn that it is merely "subjective"? But it is not destroyed. Nor is it merely subjective—no more than the Cathedral of Chartres is. Though it is a human construct, it partakes of a public world, of a collective deposit of experience and imagination; and epistemological theories about "primary" and "secondary" qualities do not destroy that world. If its details have changed—if, for example, lions and serpents have lost some of their symbolic intensity—it is not because the prevailing metaphysics has been altered but because other natural creatures (for example, mad scientists) have come, in the urban society, to share symbolic power with them. "Nature"—the living, dramatic Nature in our imaginations—reasserts itself no matter what the science or abstract metaphysics we put into our lectures. I am not sure what the disease is to which Laurence Tribe, for example, seeks a cure.

Nor do I believe that a new "faith," "myth," or "metaphysic" can be produced on demand to fill a psychic or social need, if need there be. Faiths, myths, and metaphysical doctrines do indeed come into being and win assent because they fill such needs. But the psychological fact appears to be that people must believe them to be, on independent grounds, true. The moment they realize that they believe only because it is therapeutic, useful, or expedient for them to believe, they stop believing. They recognize that they are only rationalizing, which is to recognize the absence of good grounds for belief.

X. "NATURE" AS A SYMBOL OF REASONABLENESS

I imagine it is the insensitivity of planners to the symbolic density of "Nature," together with their sometimes almost puritanical disregard for the variety of perspectives within which the meaning and value of an environmental design should be judged, that gives strength and an air of plausibility to some of the more irrationalist tendencies in the "Back-to-Nature" movement, with their celebration of the un-planned life and the multiple mysteries of existence. But it would be "unnatural" for man, not in accord with his nature as it has evolved, not to tamper with his environment or his own impulses. The choice is between different tamperings, between trying to imagine and weigh the costs of alternatives and sheer trusting to luck and prayer.

"Do what thou wilt" is the maxim by which Rabelais thought that the members of his *Abbaye de Thélème* should live. It is a hard maxim. We usually *will* incompatible things. To *do* what we will requires that we sort out our desires, investigate the conditions and likely consequences of our actions, and distinguish between what lies within our powers and what lies beyond them. In the end, perhaps the most important of all the elements of meaning in the appeal to "the rights of Nature" is that which associates "Nature" with the balanced, the circumspect, the reasonable. Values, choices, and the standards for appraising these values and choices—all these are natural events. They take place under conditions and in accordance with general laws that give us the potential, if we study them carefully enough, to see how they affect our other values, choices, and standards. By considering them to be "natural," by taking them to be on trial just as other historical products are, we may be able to make them more coherent, and thus work towards a unified notion of what it is that we will to do and be.

This is the good sense, as I see it, in the doctrine of "Natural Law," though it is not the sense, I hasten to add, that its advocates have usually emphasized. If certain goals are stipulated and certain plans are instituted to achieve these goals, the goals themselves can be treated as "natural events" and one can inquire about their connection with still other purposes, values, and events. One can always ask about a given plan whether it has been instituted within a broad enough context, or whether the time span is long enough, or whether the levels of probability of the evidence are sufficient to justify the chances being taken. In that sense, to speak of "the rights of Nature" is to utter a simple appeal to keep inquiry open and not to do things that are not justifiable in the light of the inquiries that have been taken.

We live in a world that exacts a price for whatever we do. Nothing is for free. When we say that Nature has rights we are asking what the cost is. And beyond this, we live in a world that is mysterious. No matter how much you come to know about it, it remains random, unpredictable, full of portents and fears. You see the rabbit or the deer, you live with animals who have their own vitality, and you recognize the limitations of human plans. An appeal to nature has a quasi-educational message. One is saying, "Do you want a society in which people never have the experience of living with what follows its own course, quite apart from human knowledge, desire, or hope? Do people want to build cultures and never see, in the background, things and events, processes and lives, that transcend culture, and that show that any culture is limited? Does man—educated man as much as or more than uneducated man—not need a standing warning, constantly and visibly there, reminding him of time spans that dwarf his time, of inexorabilities that mock his experiments, of fertilities that he has not set in motion?

A technological-urban environment encourages those it envelops to think that man writes his own ticket. But he is born, he matures, he dies under call. Every peasant living with Nature knows this. It is what every man knows if he will look at the Nature within him, and listen to the signals he receives each day in the beating of his heart and the rise and fall of his passions that he is an incident, a temporary collocation of energies, in a larger process. Indeed, the appeal to "Nature" may well be a useful reminder that human purposes fade, and that the sacred truths of an era are usually only collective follies. It also reminds us that, although there are laws, presumably, that explain what happens in human life, we do not know these laws and, from our partial point of view, must accept Nature as in part random, unpredictable, mysterious. So it is that the experts *must* be wrong, are destined to be wrong, unless they make explicit provision for reversing their plans and hedging their bets. They will not recognize how provincial and temporary their own sense of values is; they will not see that its sources, in all probability, lie beyond their awareness. "Nature," not man, not convention, is in the driver's seat. Intelligence and knowledge must be used to steer, but attempts at steering that ignore the unpredictability of the vehicle and the limitations of human vision are bound to be comic and disastrous.

The feeling that there is so much that drops through the net of human foresight is clearly what is involved when people not directly affected by environmental plans nevertheless raise the signal, "Go slow." Planners, after all, *have* regularly missed the boat. At the meeting of the American Economic Association at the end of 1973, its new President, Walter Heller, reminded his colleagues that there was not an important practical problem with which economists were then wrestling that they anticipated ten years earlier. A man in his fifties will have lived in this century through scores of prophecies and a dozen irresistible, but now disappeared, waves of the future. He will remember unnumbered remedies and discoveries that social scientists have offered to change the world, all now discarded. Perhaps when people say "Nature has rights" they mean only to say that we ought always to have institutional protection against being carried away by temporary enthusiasms.

Nature in fact is often cruelly unbalanced. But "Nature" in principle has been a human symbol for balance and harmony. When people appeal to "Nature," they are saying, many of them, that there is variety in the world, a plurality of value systems, an awful weight of human ignorance, and that the best we can do, the best that one must not forget to do, is to allow as commodious an arrangement of interests as possible. Inarticulately, metaphorically, they are asking, "Can you take account of what you're not taking account of? Can you not bring into harmony things over which you are riding roughshod?" Like "justice," like "truth," "Nature" is a call to keep the inquiry open, to close no books on live possibilities, and to suspect—always to suspect—the reliability of the human arts and institutions on which men are staking their lives, and, more to the point, other people's lives.

NOTES

1. E. Nagel, *The Structure of Science* (New York: Harcourt Brace, 1961), p. 4.

2. Laurence H. Tribe, "Ways Not to Think About Plastic Trees," *Yale Law Journal* 83 (June 1974):1315–1348.

3. Quoted by Tribe, supra.

4. Tribe, supra.

5. Tribe, supra.

6. *Webster's New Collegiate Dictionary* (1960).

7. *The Iliad of Homer*, trans. by Richmond Lattimore (Chicago, London: University of Chicago Press, 1951) VI, lines 146–150, p. 157.

8. J.S. Mill, *On Liberty* (Garden City, N.Y.: Doubleday), Chapter III.

9. J.S. Mill, "Nature," in *Essential Works of John Stuart Mill*, ed. by Max Lerner (New York: Bantam Books, 1961, 1965), pp. 377, 381.

10. "Nature," in *Ralph Waldo Emerson, Representative Selections*, ed. by Frederic I. Carpenter (New York: American Book, 1934), p. 13.

※ Chapter Five

Environmental Decision Making: Analysis and Values

Harvey Brooks

THE POLITICAL FUNCTIONS OF ANALYSIS

In order to understand the reasons for seeking a better means of incorporating "intangible" or "fragile" values into systems analysis, it is necessary to understand the functions analysis fulfills (or might fulfill) in environmental decisions—decisions that are fundamentally political in the sense that they ultimately involve competing or conflicting values, and therefore cannot be resolved by purely "rational" (i.e., empirical and logical-deductive) means.

The usefulness of systems analysis depends on the fact that its conclusions purport to be based on a set of neutral principles that command a wider consensus than those conclusions themselves would be likely to command without a demonstration that they are logically deducible from such principles. In this sense, policy or systems analysis perform a function with respect to political-technological decisions similar to that performed by a judicial process with respect to conflicts between individuals. A court decision is accepted by the disputing parties largely because it is based on a set of rules both parties accept applied through a procedure which both parties are prepared, before knowing its outcome, to accept as unbiased.

Of course, other factors also enter into the parties' willingness to comply: a court has substantial sanctions through which it can impose large additional costs on individuals who refuse to accept its verdicts. Analogous sanctions are not normally available against contending political interests to enforce the conclusions of a policy analysis. In some cases, it has nevertheless been possible to embody in legislation rules that mandate acceptance of the outcome of a policy analysis. As Robert Dorfman explains in his essay for this volume, one of the earliest such legislative mandates was enacted for water resources projects. There, Congress legislated specific formulas for computing the costs and benefits of a project and set minimum criteria of project acceptability in terms of a benefit-cost ratio. If a project did not meet the criteria, the presumption against it was difficult to overcome, having something like the force of a judicial decision. The existence of such legislated rules tends to reduce political conflict over choices among otherwise controversial projects, largely because the very abstraction and technicality of such rules tend to remove from political visibility all projects to which they are applied.

Indeed, one of the most likely sources of demand for the inclusion of "fragile" values in systems analysis is the hope that, by formulating general rules for incorporating such values into benefit-cost calculations, the analyst can remove political "heat" from the decision maker and can thus help to mitigate confrontation between opposing interests and factions. If such a formulation were successful, it would extend the scope of neutral principles to include the application of new kinds of criteria. As the study of the Tocks Island case has shown, political decision makers do take such values into account in their final decisions even when those values are not included in the supporting analysis. From this perspective, the problem of fragile values is not so much their neglect in the decision making process as it is bringing them into a common intellectual framework with the rest of the analysis in order to remove them from the domain of value conflict in the same way that the other calculations of benefit-cost analysis have muted political conflict over the economic viability of projects.

In principle, the values labeled "fragile," "humane," or "intangible" can be included in the objective functions that are maximized in the analytic process. One can even test a variety of objective functions by assigning different relative weights to the various values or interests whose weighted sum constitutes the function to be maximized. In such cases, a particular policy alternative may turn out to dominate all others over quite a broad range of possible objective functions. The difficulty, of course, is that such a tidy calculus is possible only if one can devise a way of measuring the intangible or "soft" values in the same units as those used for the "harder" values normally studied in cost-benefit analysis. Furthermore, if different groups with an interest in a controversy assign sufficiently different weights to the constituent elements of their particular objective functions, the range of viable policy alternatives that emerges from applying the same analysis to different objective functions will be too wide, and there will be no way of proceeding further on rational principles alone.

After the study of the Tocks Island Dam proposal, one is entitled to doubt whether the program idealized above is feasible in actual controversies. As Henry Rowen and Laurence Tribe explain more fully in their respective essays in this collection, many of the values we wish to protect are not even clearly defined, and their conventional names mean dramatically different things to different participants in the process. The best that we seem able to hope for at this stage is that systems analysis may help us to measure the costs, in terms of shortfall from other more quantifiable goals (i.e., "shadow prices"), of protecting the relatively ill-defined values we care about. For example, a particular environmental protection measure may prove surprisingly costly in terms of regional economic growth; conversely, it may prove much less costly than the opponents of protective measures initially believed. Quantification of such costs can often lead to reassessment of the intangible values to which they relate, and thus to altered choices.

A second major function of analysis is that it may help us to separate debates over means from debates over ends. Ideally, analysis would enable all those potentially affected by a decision to deduce its consequences for their particular hierarchy of values and preferences. In practice, of course, things never work out as simply as that. Means and ends are not so neatly separable. Both are embedded in a logically interconnected framework that cannot be disassembled value by value or preference by preference. Moreover, values and preferences need not be simply additive. Just as the utilities of different individuals may be interdependent, so may the goals or preferences of a single individual or group. An individual's view of a deeply preferred goal may be substantially modified when he understands the consequences of its achievement for some of his other goals. He might not even be conscious of these other goals until analysis discloses that they are threatened by realization of his highest priority preference. Individual and political attention spans alike are severely limited, and can embrace only a few goals and consequences at one time. Which ones are salient at the time of a particular decision will be profoundly influenced by the context of previous events and the historical setting of public debate. Even though analysis certainly cannot sort out all these effects, it can provide a framework that gives greater continuity and consistency to the process of decision. It can provide a way of keeping a wider range of values in the focus of attention at the same time, and can thus insure at least a partial separation of arguments over means from disputes about ends.

A third (and sometimes very controversial) function of analysis is to add legitimacy in the public eye to policy decisions. This legitimization works best when the issue has relatively low salience for any particular interest group. In such a case, the public tends to accept a decision that would otherwise be seen as arbitrary, simply because that decision is presented as the consequence of analysis. In part, such acceptance simply reflects the fact that, in a society suspicious of authority in general, science remains the one legitimating process that most can agree on. Because science represents "public knowledge" in the sense of Ziman,[1] its results can in principle be checked by anyone who cares to take enough trouble, regardless of his antecedent values. Because he trusts that the steps are reproducible, he seldom actually bothers to check them. He accepts the conclusions of analysis just as he accepts the value of paper money whose convertibility to gold is seldom tested in practice—so long as there is general trust in the proposition that it *could* be tested if necessary.

When a particular issue reaches high political salience, even if only among special elites, the legitimating function of analysis loses its force. Affected interests will attack the premises or even the techniques of the analysis and will attempt to alter its terms. Often, redefinition of criteria will rebias an analysis in favor of the particular interest or value preference which caused the issue to rise to political salience in the first place. Environmental groups have made effective use of section 102 of the National Environmental Policy Act to alter the terms of analysis for a whole series of major technological projects.[2] The starting point of the project underlying this volume was a desire to alter the terms of analysis of environmental policy issues so as to give greater weight to intangible values. To the extent that such values can be assigned "shadow prices" or be otherwise quantified, the process further legitimates the resulting outcome. It is also true, of course, that the legitimacy provided by analysis can be specious. Mountains of facts and equations can be used, either out of organizational habit or inertia or deliberately, to obfuscate more fundamental issues and to lend the authority of apparent objectivity to decisions made on unacceptable grounds, such as bureaucratic self-interest.

A fourth important function of analysis in the political process occurs when it succeeds in converting apparent zero-sum games into positive-sum games—i.e., when it discloses solutions to a conflict that satisfy all the parties, if not completely, at least more than they intuitively anticipated was possible. Very often analysis helps to reveal new possibilities, to widen the range of policy choices available. Moreover, as a fifth function, analysis can frequently eliminate from consideration alternatives that are "dominated" by other alternatives, i.e., that are worse no matter what relative weight is given to the various interests or values at issue, at least over a fairly wide range. When analysis succeeds in doing this unambiguously, it becomes a very powerful (and a wholly legitimate) tool of political persuasion.

None of these functions of analysis is entirely separable from the others. The legitimation function is important, for example, because it helps in consensus forming. The shift of the debate from means to consequences can either contribute to or detract from consensus, depending upon circumstances. A clearer understanding and exposition of consequences can expose fundamental value differences that were previously glossed over in the debate over specific means. A consensus on a specific line of action may evaporate when all its consequences are more fully understood. Groups may oppose or favor a specific project for widely differing reasons, and thus form an effective political coalition that would be eroded by more explicit analysis. On the other hand, groups may modify their support or opposition to specific projects when the social costs of achieving their ends are more explicitly set out. In short, analysis can stimulate the reevaluation of values through better understanding of their practical implications, and can change the terms of social valuation, not by operating directly on the values themselves but by clarifying the implications of some values for other values within a single individual's or group's framework of ends.

THE VALUATION OF NATURE

One of the principal problems of incorporating intangible values in analysis arises from their incomplete or ambiguous definition and articulation. Groups with different perspectives may use the same words for values that represent quite different domains of subjective experience and that trigger quite different subjective images. This is, after all, why we call them intangible. The words are not names for entities of "public knowledge" and are thus unlike "harder" values, which can be given more operational definitions. Thus an essential aspect of dealing rationally with intangible or fragile values is the attempt to reduce them to more operational terms.

As industrial societies have grown more complex and more

affluent, an increasing fraction of the population has come to live in cities. And many city dwellers, because of their mobility, have potential access to nature, including those resources that are both unique and finite—namely, primitive nature and unspoiled wilderness. Many of these areas are such that, the more people use them, the less attractive and valuable they become to those who do have access to them. It is only natural that our cultural valuation of wilderness should increase rapidly as the prospect of its degradation arising from other human uses becomes more widespread. Pristine nature becomes more valuable simply because the demand for it is constantly increasing while the supply is decreasing, both effects being products of industrial civilization. Thus much of the valuation placed on nature is simply a result of its scarcity in a strictly economic sense. But the natural environment is much harder to ration than other scarce goods. For cultural reasons we look upon it as part of the common heritage of all, rather than as something to be rationed by the market alone, accessible to an ever-narrowing minority of the rich as its value increases. In this sense, it partakes of many of the properties of a "merit good" as defined by Musgrave.[3]

Although we must therefore struggle for ways of rationing nature politically rather than economically, we know of no "just" way to do this, giving equal access to all who want it. Uses of nature that benefit many people, including its destruction for economic purposes, are increasingly condemned by society acting collectively. The reason is that the natural environment is felt by many to have an intrinsic value, a value that (incidentally) benefits even those who do not enjoy or benefit from it in any direct way. A majestic piece of scenery, or a unique ecosystem, enhances the quality of a society which possesses and cherishes it just as surely as does a national historical monument, a great work of art, or a cathedral.

In modern societies at least, our valuation of nature is intimately related to our capacity to understand it and to describe it in scientific terms. It is probably no coincidence that the movement to assert the values of nature has been spearheaded by the scientists who understand nature best, and have devoted their lives to its study. The "rights of nature" is a human construct; as Charles Frankel reminds us, the construct represents an effort to institutionalize protection against our being carried away by temporary enthusiasms of exploitation, and against our acting with overconfidence in our ability to foresee the potential consequences. Thus notions such as the "rights of nature" or "fragile values" have a social function analogous to that of taboos or religious beliefs in more traditional cultures. They are, in large part, a surrogate for reasoned collective decisions, a bow to the complexity we have not yet mastered and must therefore not disturb too much.

One reason such a surrogate is needed is that we possess no scale of values for nature that can be readily weighed in the balance against the fulfillment of man's material needs or desires. To a degree, of course, nature does embody values that are of the same kind we use in computing material benefits. For example, we say that the preservation of nature protects resources for the future, including future generations. The protection of a natural ecosystem is an economic investment for the sake of a future benefit just as assuredly as the development of a mine or the conduct of a research and development program. We can go a long way, at least in principle if not in practice, in treating nature like any other economic investment for a future stream of economic benefits. Even if we are not knowledgeable enough to quantify these future benefits deterministically, we can regard the preservation of nature in the same light as an insurance premium, a hedge against future events or conditions we cannot now foresee. There are many who would argue that this is the only reasonable basis on which to value nature—i.e., that economic self-interest, viewed in the longest range and most sophisticated terms to embrace our descendants as well as ourselves, is a sufficient criterion in principle for incorporating intangible and fragile values in our analysis. If we know very little about the full ramifications of our present interventions in the natural environment, the conventional calculus of decision under uncertainty may suffice to justify at least part of our ecological caution even in the most cold-blooded economic terms.

To whatever extent such economic analysis falls short of making a convincing case for ecological caution, the case remains an appealing one on other grounds. History teaches us that much of the folklore and mythology of the past had an important social function in enabling humanity to cope with environmental complexity it could not scientifically understand. Yet recent science has frequently confirmed the empirical basis at the core of folk wisdom, and it is possible that some future historian will see our romantic views of nature as having served a similar purpose during the age of exploding affluence and material exploitation. Thus we may consider that we are in a sort of transition period in which our analytical capability, and the state of our empirical knowledge, cannot be used in support of a political function for analysis of certain difficult questions, such as the importance of preserving nature.

Rather we must content ourselves with vaguer principles, expressed in terms of values that have something of a mystical and romantic sound, and that have more in common with traditional taboos and folklore than with rational arguments. However, as our knowledge increases we must be prepared for the fact that some of the previous bases for ecological caution will disappear, and others may be intensified. Ignorance or uncertainty cannot be used indefinitely as a persuasive basis for ecological decision making. We cannot assume that folk wisdom and ethical tradition will necessarily be confirmed by scientific knowledge in the future.

Putting aside the preceding speculations, I think we can discern certain themes in our valuations of nature which it is possible to formulate fairly precisely, even if not quantitatively. Examples of such implicit criteria of valuation are the following:

1. *Uniqueness.* Natural systems that are not duplicated elsewhere have a higher value than those that are more widely distributed. It was the fact that the Delaware was the last free-flowing river in the heart of the industrialized East which gave the Tocks Island Dam project special significance in the eyes of environmentalists, and helped mobilize opposition to it.

2. *Reversibility or resilience.* Actions that are irreversible, or reversible only at huge cost, should carry a much heavier burden of proof than actions that may affect unique and beautiful, but relatively resilient, environments. An oil pipeline across the permafrost regions of Alaska justifiably arouses more alarm than the bulldozing of a fine beech forest in rural Virginia. The beech forest is a sad loss, but it will grow back some day if we change our minds, whereas the disturbance of the permafrost *may* trigger a progressive chain reaction of deterioration that we can never stop, as for example did the overgrazing of the hills of North Africa. At least it is this belief that conditions many of our attitudes, whether or not it is actually valid. The Corps of Engineers, in the Tocks case, recognized this point of view even if only with tongue in cheek when it argued that the Tocks Island Dam could be removed at some later time if that proved necessary.

3. *Beauty.* An important component of society's valuation of nature is esthetic. No less than a human artifact, natural beauty is a culture object. Tastes in nature change just as do tastes in art or music, though some tastes are more permanent than others, and the most majestic and awesome spectacles of nature, such as the Grand Canyon, seem to have an almost universal and timeless appeal.

4. *Human life support.* This is the aspect of nature that, in principle, is most easily subject to analysis in the same terms as material benefits and costs. Thus, for example, the preservation of wild genetic stocks of major food plants may be essential at some time in the future for the restoration, through breeding, of agricultural monocultures attacked by new varieties of pathogens or pests. The protection of the ecology of coastal estuaries that play a part in the life cycle of oceanic fish stocks may be essential to maintenance of marine fisheries. Thus the value of a particular feature of nature as part of the future human habitat becomes one of the criteria for its preservation or restoration.

5. *Naturalness.* This is an especially elusive criterion, but one that nevertheless seems to play an important part in debates over natural preservation. A part of nature that evolves free of any human intervention whatever is regarded as having a special value in its own right. A piece of undisturbed nature is more valuable than an equally attractive natural system maintained by human cultivation. This has not always been so; it represents a distinctively modern attitude probably brought about by the increasing rarity of truly natural environments, and by the growing sense that people need *something* in their environments that is not of their own making or shaping, if only because they would be lost in a universe that simply mirrored themselves (see Laurence Tribe's essay in this volume). The attitude is illustrated by the recent change in approach to the control of forest fires. In many areas, firefighting is now regarded as an undesirable human intervention in the natural succession of the forest ecosystem. To some extent this change in approach to forest fires may have an objective scientific basis, but it is also to a considerable extent the result of an emotional reaction to any interference with the "natural order of things." Clearly in the case of Tocks, the wild river was seen as having a special value arising from its "naturalness," a feature that would have been valued even if it could be demonstrated that an artificial lake could have been made more beautiful. To some extent this intrinsic valuation of naturalness can be traced back to what I have said about preservation of nature as insurance against human ignorance, against the unpredictable consequences of intervention, but I believe that the feeling goes deeper than any justification one could develop in purely rational terms.

These five criteria for the valuation of nature are not entirely independent of one another. Naturalness and uniqueness both contribute to our sense of beauty, for example. Naturalness and reversibility both relate to the preservation of future human life support. Beauty of natural surroundings may be essential to the future psychological well-being of humanity. Nevertheless, each of the criteria has a distinct identity in the public debates over preservation. There is no independent, rational basis for assigning a price to such criteria in a cost-benefit analysis, but defining the criteria is an important first step that can aid analysis by permitting testing of the impact of various assigned prices. For example, it should be possible to assign a scale of values to uniqueness, though different groups may disagree about the dollar value of a unit on the scale, so that the scale may be expanded or contracted in the eyes of different beholders.

PROJECT ASSESSMENT VS. PROBLEM ASSESSMENT

It is difficult to fault analysis for its failure to deal with "intangible" values when, even in its own "hard-headed" terms, it is poorly done. For example, in the case of the Tocks Island Dam, the most striking characteristic of the analysis is its poor and incomplete character even when judged in the narrowest terms. One does not have to invoke "humane" values to justify serious reconsideration of the Tocks proposal; there may be no deficiency in the decision or in the analysis that a good "technical fix" would not cure. Robert Dorfman lets the cat out of the bag when he admits "there are such technical difficulties in the design of the project that it seems unlikely to work out as idyllically as described in the text," after a glowing description of a Sunday outing of a "poor or near-poor" family from New York or Philadelphia. (See his essay in this volume.)

Many of the faults of the Tocks Island decision process can be related to an inadequate choice of the boundaries of the system to be studied. The analysis was a project-oriented assessment rather than a problem-oriented assessment. It looked at each of the different problems to whose solution Tocks might contribute, but it did not search widely for the optimum way of dealing with any single one of those problems. Those problems included flood control, water supply, energy supply, salinity control, and recreation. In computing the benefits from a multipurpose, single-technology project such as Tocks, one is too likely to overlook alternative solutions to each of the separate "problems" represented by each purpose. In addition, the baseline against which the benefits of the project are measured is vague, since we do not know what would have happened in the absence of the project, for example, under the influence of market forces alone. Would the uncoordinated development of second homes, condominiums, and private recreation facilities end by being more damaging to the environment of the area than a planned recreation area or than the dam? The comparison of costs and benefits is not properly between the project in question and an unchanged environment, yet this appears to be the way it was implicitly evaluated. Would the rigid control of local development have been the actual policy alternative chosen if the Tocks project had been rejected by the voters?

In the case of flood protection, there are many other alternatives for achieving such protection, including flood-plain zoning, properly designed flood insurance, and quick-reaction warning and prediction systems.[4] Still other alternatives are possible, such as controls on the upper watershed and tributaries, high-flow skimming, and the like. High-flow skimming has been mentioned in connection with water supply, but it can have flood control implications as well.

Thus, before one can readily apply multipurpose analysis to a case such as Tocks, one should really carry out a series of single-purpose problem analyses for each of the problem areas mentioned above, with the system boundaries for each problem carefully chosen to take into account a number of possible external interactions. This may imply a different system boundary for each problem, as well as consideration of alternate ways of drawing the boundary.

The way the water supply question has been dealt with in the Tocks case offers many examples in which failure to consider external interactions resulted in arbitrary and unjustified assumptions in the analysis—e.g., the diversion of upper Delaware water to the New York City water supply, the failure to consider leaks and wastage in the New York City system, the failure to consider ground water as an emergency source of low-flow augmentation, the failure to consider recycling of water as an alternative to dissipative use, the failure to consider alternative locations for power plants to make less consumptive use of fresh water.[5] Even in hard-headed economic terms, many of these alternatives might have offered benefits greater than those of the Tocks investment, without any worry about "humane" values. As Robert Socolow has emphasized, the boundary conditions of analysis are often chosen to fit into political constraints of long standing, whose origins are so far in the past that nobody remembers the rationale for them.

Almost all the problem areas to which the Tocks project purports to be addressed have been incompletely analyzed. There has never been a truly comprehensive study of the recreational requirements for the metropolitan areas of New York and Philadelphia, an analysis that included transportation requirements, and that took into account the changing educational levels and tastes of the populations involved. The National Academy of Sciences' study of Jamaica Bay, for example, disclosed many possibilities for recreational development much closer to the metropolitan area,[6] but no analysis of Tocks ever compared the project with these alternatives. There has apparently never been a comprehensive study of the future energy requirements of the Delaware Basin region that takes into account conservation possibilities, alternative forms of power plant cooling, and the possibilities of importation of energy from outside the region.

The feedback between population and industrial growth on the one hand, and the provision of infrastructure facilities such as power, water, and transportation on the other, has apparently never been factored into regional development studies. On the contrary, growth of population and industry have been treated as exogenous variables, and the needed infrastructure has been calculated on this basis without considering the degree to which provision of this infrastructure would accelerate development or its absence would retard regional growth. The ground water system of the region has never been fully explored, and seems not to have been taken into account in the assessment of the region's water supply. Even the carefully computed recreational benefits of the Tocks reservoir are subject to large uncertainties arising from the possible eutrophication of the reservoir as a consequence of upstream agricultural activities, and no adequate program to resolve these uncertainties has been developed.

The eutrophication problem could invalidate the whole economic analysis of the recreation benefits, which is predicated on water quality in the reservoir adequate for boating, swimming, and other water centered recreation activities. The situation is similar to that which occurred in the case of the sonic boom problem in connection with the SST: much of the economic analysis on which the assessment of the SST was based depended on the assumption that overland flights would not be precluded by adverse public reactions to the boom. What these examples suggest is that it is important to establish priorities for analysis in order to avoid elaborate investigations based on assumptions vulnerable to invalidation by adequate analysis of other parts of the problem. There are hierarchies of topics for analysis that must be respected if the analysis process is not to be wasteful and irrelevant.

The reasons for the various limitations of the Tocks analysis are, of course, implicit in the history and politics of the issue. Many assumptions in the analysis were locked in by previous legal or political commitments, and simply became rigid and arbitrary constraints that made no sense in a more comprehensive context. As Irene Thomson observes in her essay in this volume, the different political decision makers had quite different perceptions of the issue, depending on how the costs could be expected to fall on their own particular political constituencies. Certain numbers, such as the 3,000 cfs low-flow requirement at Trenton, acquired the status of unexaminable premises and were used to provide urgent justification for the 3000 cfs flow to be assured by the Tocks Island Dam. This was because the Delaware was considered as a closed system, with external boundary conditions that could not be modified or relaxed. The hidden agenda of each of the analytical groups led it, perhaps unconsciously, to structure the boundaries of the problem so as to support an outcome favorable to its bureaucratic or other unmentionable interests. The assumptions became partially unlocked only as various adversary interests entered the political picture and began to provide new analyses with assumptions slanted to generate outcomes that favored their own a priori preferences. Biased analysis highlighted the unconscious biases in earlier analyses, if only by providing contrast.

Why should the various actors be so shy about "fragile" values, concealing them under apparently hard-headed analysis carefully predesigned so that the outcome would favor their unacknowledged values? The reason is essentially political. In the American polity, hard-headed arguments have usually been more effective in achieving consensus than arguments deriving from very generally stated national goals. If an alternative can be eliminated from consideration on the basis of technico-economic arguments, it is less necessary to argue from premises on which different social groups are likely to differ profoundly, such as growth vs. equilibrium. On the other side, consensus objectives, if they do exist, are usually stated so generally and abstractly that neither the public nor the decision maker can translate them into concrete policies on real issues. For example, nobody will overtly argue against fragile values; they will simply behave as though they were not relevant to the particular decision at hand.

I suspect that, as one extends the boundaries of the system with respect to which policy analysis is conducted, the difference in outcome between hard-headed analysis and analysis that takes greater account of humane values may narrow. I cannot prove this, but until analysis is conducted in the broadest possible terms, it seems to be a good working hypothesis. As the boundaries widen, the effects of an action on more and more people are included, and it is more likely that new values will be introduced into the analysis. As I have suggested in the section on the valuation of nature, a proper consideration of the need to preserve the future human habitat or of the psychosocial benefits of exposure to unspoiled nature may be sufficient to justify protection without appealing to more intangible arguments.

The undesired outcomes of the incomplete and partial analyses so far put forward are not convincing evidence that it is necessary to find ways of quantifying fragile values. The problem at present seems to be that analysts are more constrained than they are willing to admit by the political and social presuppositions of the milieu in which they work. Indeed, their own professional commitment to the value of analysis tends to blind them to these constraints. Much cost-benefit analysis seems to be conducted by economists and engineers with a trained incapacity to appreciate political factors, and indeed a contempt for politics as somehow an unreal and artificial constraint outside the real world of hydraulic flows and dollars. The main function of the injection of new values into the analysis (as by environmental groups, for example) is to catalyze a widening of the terms of analysis, the range of alternatives, and the boundaries of the system to be analyzed. They are just that, catalysts that promote better analysis, rather than necessary ingredients.

THE BURDEN OF PROOF

There has been a real change in the climate of public opinion, which has shifted the burden of proof as between the advocates of growth and development and the advocates of restraint. The deployment of new technology, or new public or private investments, is now increasingly regarded as potentially deleterious until proved harmless, whereas formerly it was considered innocent until proved damaging.[7] Much more weight is attached now than in the past to the preservation of options for the future; society is more inclined to favor actions that can be changed or reversed in the light of new knowledge or experience as compared with actions that involve less easily reversible long term commitments. In fact, the identification of "irreversible commitments" is one of the criteria explicitly mentioned in the requirements for the environmental impact statements mandated in NEPA.[8] Thus flood-plain zoning may be inherently preferable to large scale dams because future policy can be adjusted in the light of experience.

Where a choice is presented between investment to make more efficient use of a resource as compared with investment in increased supply, the former is to be preferred because there is less uncertainty about its secondary effects, and the option of investing in increased supply at a later time still remains open. As the externalities of increased supply are increasingly internalized in the cost of a resource—including the environment itself—more efficient use of resources becomes more attractive economically in comparison with increasing the supply. This is true in the case of free goods such as water, clean air, flood-plain land, and, to a growing extent, other goods such as energy and materials. We are still in a transition stage within this change.

The shift of the burden of proof also leads into a rebalancing of effort between design and analysis, in favor of analysis. Many of the examples cited in our discussion of Tocks suggest that better analysis is cheap in comparison with the mistakes and unforeseen consequences resulting from permanent investment. History has demonstrated the almost total invalidity, and indeed irrelevance, of the original Corps of Engineers studies of the expected costs and benefits of Tocks. It was the shift in the burden of proof that occurred between the time of the original plan and the DRBC study that required a better analysis, and the continuing debate on the project provided the time and basis for additional study. What this shows is that much effort devoted to detailed design of concrete projects can be wasted if detailed project design is not preceded by a comprehensive and wide ranging but relatively general assessment of the potential effects of the project and of alternative approaches to the problems that the project was intended to solve. Much of the analytical effort devoted to design might better be devoted, at least initially, to assessment and the approximate exploration of a wide variety of options, rather than to the detailed design of a few.

PARTICIPATORY DECISION MAKING

During recent years there has been a sudden upsurge in emphasis on the importance of public participation in decisions about the application or deployment of technology. Laurence Tribe's essay takes the view that the process by which a result is arrived at is often at least as important as the result itself, so that one cannot judge the value of a decision by looking at its outcome alone. Some advocates of participatory decision making indeed appear to believe that the process is far more important than the outcome—that in fact there is no truly independent way of judging an outcome other than by judging the process by which it was reached.

Now process *is* very important. This is so in part because the choices involved in a project such as Tocks are to a certain extent dependent on the surrounding culture, and cannot be made entirely on the basis of strictly rational or even easily articulated criteria. To the extent that the ultimate criteria of choice are intangible and unquantifiable, it is only the process of choice that can validate or legitimize the outcome in the eyes of society. In this sense it is really the process that defines the criteria, and even quantifies them after the fact. Indeed, the outcome of any choice that involves unquantifiable elements implicitly quantifies these elements. Society's choice of speed limits and the costs it is willing to accept for safety features in automobile and highway design represent implicit valuations of human life and suffering from auto accidents.

It is for this reason that I agree with Robert Dorfman on the necessity for a disciplined process of making major decisions about the deployment of technology, with rigorous standards governing the admissibility of arguments and evidence and determining what interests and representatives have standing in the process. The purpose of Dorfman's court should be in part to allocate analytical resources among relevant interests, including those that represent "elite," or "intangible," or "fragile" values. There are obvious difficulties, however, with the normal political process: it is disorderly and undisciplined, and it provides insufficient guarantees that all the relevant values and interests will be considered. Furthermore, present processes often invite paralysis in the resolution of issues.

In the United States, political preference has tended to alternate between political participation and professional management. When the public at large becomes disgusted with the paralysis of decision making occasioned by excessive deference to parochial interests and political logrolling, it opts for the technocrats; when it becomes disillusioned with the arbitrary and impersonal power of the technocrats, it opts for greater participation. The early days of the Kennedy administration represented the high water mark of public confidence in experts and professionals and the willingness to believe that the major problems facing America could be attacked with technical and administrative skills that were largely "apolitical." Arthur Schlesinger quotes Kennedy as saying that the real issue at that time (1963) was the management of industrial society—a problem not of ideology but of administration.[9]

But just as the intellectuals were proclaiming the end of ideology, the public began to swing away from this position. New constituencies began to be heard from who regarded expertise and professionalism as camouflage for the preservation of existing power relations. The Vietnam War was seen as a war made by technocrats, its shots called by experts who accepted as an unexamined premise U.S. national interest in the preservation of the South Vietnam regime as a bulwark against communism, and who were concerned with the most effective political, economic, military, and technological means to that end. The revolt against this technocratic style of decision making rapidly spread to all phases of the political process. In part it represented a generational change. It seems likely, however, that we are now in an extreme swing of a reaction towards "open" government, and that we will look back on the present period with some of the same feeling of amazement and rejection that many of us now feel towards the years 1955–65.

The present emphasis on participatory decision making (the opposite of technocratic decision making) is a reaction not only against Vietnam but also against the technically oriented public authorities with minimal political accountability who were so much a feature of public works projects in the 1930s and 1940s (and to some extent even into the 1950s). What currently fashionable participatory decision making is *against* is clearly and graphically described in a series of four articles by R.A. Caro on Robert Moses and his control of public works in New York City that appeared in *The New Yorker*.[10] In Caro's words:

> . . . Moses was not responsible to the public. Its votes had not put him in office, and its votes could not remove him from office. He despised its opinion. The considerations that he took into account were the considerations that mattered to him personally: the project, in and for itself; the engineering considerations that would get it done the fastest and cheapest way; and the economic considerations that mattered to the forces he was using to impose his will on the city.

To a considerable extent policy analysis as practiced in the Tocks case was in this tradition. Indeed, the project was caught in the transition from the climate of opinion that made possible the situation caricatured in the career of Robert Moses to an entirely new situation—one caricatured by the legal battles and court decisions surrounding the siting of nuclear power plants in the late 1960s.

A central question, of course, is whether the new mode of

participatory decision making is any more viable than was the old one of engineering and economic autocracy. The Moses system, like the traditions of the Corps of Engineers, "got things done," but that system was almost totally unresponsive to the public in any specific way. The new system is more responsive to the public—or at least to some publics—but there is grave doubt as to whether it can get things done. The twelve years of Tocks have not led to any final resolution of the issues, but have simply delayed decision time after time. While there is no question that participatory decision making can stop, and has stopped, possibly undesirable projects, it remains to be seen whether it can ever initiate desirable or needed actions involving the positive use of technology in the public interest.

The case has been well made for the value of adversary analysis in bringing new considerations and perspectives into the decision making process; in the case of Tocks, it prevented the acceptance of analyses that proved in retrospect to be seriously flawed, even from a strictly technocratic standpoint. It produced a pause for reflection, which in this case was almost certainly desirable. To this extent, wider public participation was a virtue. But I have yet to hear of an example in which public participation in the sense desired by its advocates has accelerated a technological project that was badly needed.

The participatory process gives unusual leverage to local or parochial interests that are adversely affected by a project, whereas more diffuse and generalized benefits tend to go unrepresented unless the public benefit happens also to be beneficial to a powerful economic interest, such as a public utility or a construction union. Such economic interests have been widely discredited in recent years; their interests are usually assumed to be contrary to "the public interest" by definition, though there is no inherent logic that dictates that this must be so. Of course, the power of local interests is enhanced when assessments are made in terms of projects rather than problems: it is easier to mobilize opposition to a particular project whose victims are well identified but whose beneficiaries are not so clearly defined. It would probably have been easier to generate a wide consensus on the need for additional recreation facilities for metropolitan residents in the mid Atlantic region, and then to decide later on the most appropriate character and locations for such facilities rather than put forward one option and justify it by its recreational benefits, almost as an afterthought.

One has to be cautious, however, in discussing the meaning of political accountability. It is true that Robert Moses rode roughshod over the rights and preferences of many local communities and neighborhoods, but he enjoyed immense political popularity and prestige with the New York State electorate as a whole, and few local politicians dared oppose his projects publicly. If a referendum had been conducted on his far-flung activities, he would almost certainly have won it hands down, because he was regarded as being "for progress," and was moving in step with the broad political currents of his time. This is so despite the fact that much of his power was exercised behind closed doors, and that he was not above using strong-arm tactics and thinly disguised bribery to keep local politicians as his allies and supporters. "Buying off" parochial interests in order to defuse opposition to projects deemed by many to be in the larger public interest has been a standard technique of successful technocrats, though seldom acknowledged publicly.

Advocacy of participatory decision making inevitably raises the questions: Who should participate? How should the participants be identified? The central argument in favor of technocracy was always that technocrats could consider the broad public good, unpressured by special interests and random political winds. Today we are more aware that technocrats have their own axes to grind, that they are not intrinsically more selfless or dedicated to the public weal than is the average politician; it is just that they have different axes to grind. They are not outside the political game; they are a part of it.

The ultimate difficulty with participatory decision processes is the lack of assurance that all the relevant interests and perspectives will be represented in a balanced way. Mobilization of a particular affected constituency may depend on accidents of leadership or of command over financial resources. Many affected groups may not even perceive that their interests are involved. Others may be young children, or unborn future generations. As many have stressed, people's needs and wants are not givens, but depend (among other things) on their knowledge of what is possible or available. Thus the attempts of analysts empirically to discover social goals by means of surveys or by indirect inference from social behavior were doomed to inadequacy from the start. Moreover, as Laurence Tribe and Robert Dorfman have emphasized, consumer preferences and political priorities are highly subject to manipulation or conditioning and thus cannot be regarded as "given," even if the current techniques for discovering them were less technically flawed.

What seems to be called for at this stage is a new synthesis of the participatory and technocratic styles. Indeed it is just this sort of synthesis that seems to be envisioned in the procedure proposed by Dorfman, an effort to cope with the undisciplined nature of participatory decision making as currently practiced. But I think a two-stage process is necessary. The first stage I envision would be much as Dorfman proposed it: a number of adversary analyses would be presented, with allocation of budgets for the analytical work being the responsibility of some neutral, quasi-judicial body. But who is to sort out the adversary analyses? The busy "decision maker" (who is really plural, as Dorfman says) surely lacks both the time and the attention span necessary to evaluate complex and conflicting studies, and the general public or its self-appointed spokesmen are not qualified to do so.

There needs to be an institution something like a technical-analytical court, an organization with the technical competence to deal with the various adversary analyses on their own terms, comparing their assumptions, their formulations of the problem, their methodology, the boundaries of their analyses, and their data. In the language of technology assessment, the institution needed is an assessor of assessors,[11] although what I have in mind is more disciplined than what has been contemplated in the technology assessment literature. Part of the objective of this second-stage assessment would be to clarify and explain the choices before the public—or, more accurately, before the various publics potentially affected by the decision. I would not urge that this clarification be intended fully to depoliticize the process of decision, or that it be designed to effect a complete separation of means and ends. I would urge it as a second approximation to such a separation, a stage beyond traditional policy analysis.

Of course the accountable decision makers in the political realm will (and should continue to) make the final decisions, but they ought to have available to them not only the raw data and analyses. They ought also to have available a simplified and summarized analysis that is a critique of the technically sophisticated analyses produced by the many adversaries addressing the issue. In this way, one might realistically hope simultaneously to optimize the political role played by analysis itself; to strike a wise balance between problem and project assessment; to draw on the strengths of both the technocratic and political modes of decision; and to move toward a balanced and sensitive allocation of the many burdens of uncertainty, both factual and normative, that necessarily beset our halting efforts to arrive at appropriate valuations of nature.

NOTES

1. John M. Ziman, *Public Knowledge, the Social Dimension of Science* (Cambridge: Cambridge University Press, 1968).

2. A. W. Murphy, "NEPA and the Licensing Process: Environmentalist Magna Carta or Agency Coup de Grace?" *Columbia Law Review* 72 (6)(October 1972):963.

3. Richard Musgrave, "On Social Goods and Social Bads," chap. 9, p. 251 in R. Marris, ed., *The Corporate Society* (New York: Macmillan, 1974).

4. Allan S. Krass, "Flood Control and the Tocks Island Dam," *Boundaries of Analysis* (Cambridge, Mass.: Ballinger, 1976). Robert Socolow also discusses some of these alternatives in his essay in this book.

5. Frank W. Sinden, "Water Supply and the Tocks Island Dam," *Boundaries of Analysis* (Cambridge, Mass.: Ballinger, 1976). See Robert Socolow's essay in this book also.

6. *Jamaica Bay and Kennedy Airport, A Multidisciplinary Environmental Study*, 2 vols., (Washington, D.C.: National Academy of Sciences–National Academy of Engineering, 1971), ISPN 0-309-01871-4, L. C. No. 78-610437.

7. NAS, *Technology: Processes of Assessment and Choice*, Report of the National Academy of Sciences to the Committee on Science and Astronautics, U.S. House of Representatives, July 1969 (Washington, D.C.: U.S. Government Printing Office, 1969), p. 33.

8. The National Environmental Policy Act of 1969, sec. 102.

9. Arthur Schlesinger, Jr., *A Thousand Days*, (Boston: Houghton Mifflin, 1965), p. 644.

10. R. A. Caro, "The Power Broker, III: How Things Get Done," *The New Yorker*, August 12, 1974.

11. NAS, *Technology: Processes of Assessment and Choice*, p. 91.

Chapter Six

Policy Analysis as Heuristic Aid:
The Design of Means,
Ends, and Institutions

Henry S. Rowen

"Policy analysis" refers to a set of procedures for inventing, exploring, and comparing the alternatives available for achieving certain social ends—and for inventing, exploring, and comparing the alternative ends themselves—in a world limited in knowledge, in resources and in rationality. Policy analysts use scientific data and theories as inputs, employ the method of science in many of their procedures, and sometimes stimulate the creation of new fundamental knowledge, but theirs is not a science. Rather, it is a profession—possibly a bit beyond the state of medicine early in this century, when Lawrence J. Henderson asserted that the average patient who came into contact with the average physician stood an even chance of benefiting from the encounter.

I

Policy analysis can be put to many uses. It can be used to help make routine decisions (e.g., the optimization of a system for responding to fire alarms) and to help make decisions on nonroutine events (e.g., the structuring of the main features of a national health insurance system). It can be used to raise questions about, and explore the consistency among, objectives of the same or different government programs (e.g., programs to increase irrigated agricultural land versus programs that remove land from cultivation). It can be employed in advocacy against competition (e.g., by the Air Force and Navy on the merits of their respective strategic nuclear forces). It can provide nonmembers of powerful bureaucracies (e.g., political appointees) with arguments against some of these bureaucracies' programs at the same time that it helps the bureaucracies to fight back. And it can point to directions for seeking new knowledge that might eventually contribute to solving policy problems (e.g., the effect of environmental stimulation on early childhood development). Policy analysis can be used in all of these many ways, and, in its now quite substantial history, it has been so used.

Policy analysts therefore play many roles. They are staff advisors to decision makers, or may even be decision makers themselves with their thinking caps on. They are members of career services. They can also be found in firms which sell analytic services. Important concentrations of them are to be found in research institutions and universities. Theirs is a peripatetic community. The diffusion of ideas and methods is greatly promoted by the movement of analysts from place to place. They bring or develop subject area expertise, institutional knowledge, quantitative analytic skills, problem solving skills, and occasionally skills in communicating the nature and validity of their findings to decision makers and wider audiences.

In some of these roles, analysts are overtly partisan; in others less so. (Wherever they are located, many analysts have some values that do not correspond in any obvious way to those of the institutional setting in which they work.) But it is not required that analysts be completely nonpartisan, assuming that we could identify zero on a scale of partisanship. Analysts need be no more neutral in their fields nor saintly in their character than are contributors to pure science. But whatever the appearance or reality of partisanship, what matters is the work done and the applicable standard of evaluation is that of the scientific method: careful use of data, explicitness in stating assumptions and the production of replicable calculations. Moreover, partisanship has social value because it can be a motivator of discoveries that affect policy choices. "Blowing the opposition out of the water" may not be the most noble of motives but it may have useful social consequences.

With so varied a set of purposes and players, what, if anything, can be said about the characteristics of good analysis? In my view, good analysis does the following:

1. Uses methods tailored to the character of the problem and the nature of the data; treats data skeptically.
2. Explores, reformulates, and invents objectives; recognizes the multiplicity of the objectives that are held; recognizes hierarchies of objectives and the fact that one is always working on intermediate objectives.

3. Uses criteria of choice sensitively and with caution, giving weight to qualitative as well as quantitative factors.
4. Emphasizes the design and invention of alternatives; tries to avoid concentration on too narrow a set of alternatives.
5. Handles uncertainty explicitly.
6. Evidences that the analyst understands the central technical facts of the problem.
7. Uses simple models to illuminate important aspects of the problem and avoids large models that purport to represent much of reality but that conceal the basic structure of the problem and uncertainties among parameters.
8. Displays truth in labeling of assumptions, values, uncertainties, hypotheses, and conjectures.
9. Shows understanding that the task is usually not to optimize but only to find better alternatives.
10. Shows that an effort has been made to understand decision makers' problems and constraints especially if the analyst proposes a radical reformulation of the problem.
11. Tries to take into account the organizational factors that shape the alternatives generated and influence the outcomes of decisions.
12. Exhibits awareness of the usefulness of partial analysis and of the limits of analysis generally.

This may seem counsel of perfection. If institutional arrangements invariably provided for review, criticism and counteranalysis of analytic work, these characteristics would be more in evidence than they are. Indeed, it might be argued that although no single analysis is likely to exhibit all of the desirable properties listed above, the corpus of analytic work done on a problem over time may approximate this ideal. This may leave uncomfortable those who, although rejecting the model of decision makers as philosopher-kings, conceive of policy analysts as philosopher advisors to kings. I am inclined to see analysts in a more modest role, equipped with certain tools, and subject, intermittently and imperfectly, to certain standards of performance, and therefore to place more reliance on a competitive analytic process.

Points 2 and 3 from this list, concerning objectives, criteria and the handling of qualitative factors, have been central to our project and deserve particular attention. These are not just matters of analytic technique; they are intimately connected to ways we form preferences and to the role of performance indicators in our institutional structures. I will return to this topic later.

II

Robert Dorfman's essay in this volume traces the historical evolution of policy analysis from maximization under constraint, through recognition of the importance of choosing the objective function, to a greater concern about values. Clearly there has been an evolution along these lines, but this characterization gives insufficient emphasis to what I believe have been two principal contributions of this line of work: clarification of issues, and the design and invention of objectives and alternatives. This view is in marked contrast to the emphasis placed on optimization and evaluation in the literature on this subject. It is not that the latter are not useful, indeed often necessary, activities, but that the payoffs from the former are so much greater. As Edward Quade has put it, "A good new idea is worth a thousand evaluations." (But a good evaluation may be a condition for getting a good idea.) More fundamentally, this view is based on the observation that those responsible for policy choices often do not have a clear concept of what needs to be done, are not in possession of the relevant facts, do not know the alternatives available and do not know, even approximately, the consequences of choosing particular courses of action. Let us refer to someone in this state of mind as being in Position A.[1]

The salient facts about Position A are these:

First, often those responsible for making public policy decisions do not have clearly articulated or well defined preferences among broad goals nor preferences among specific policy objectives. One reason is that the policy issues involved often concern public goods—goods not sold on markets. The value placed on these goods by members of the community is largely unknown because they have few occasions to obtain information on what these goods are worth to them or what they cost. This is also true in the related phenomenon of spillovers from private actions, if the effects are diffused among large numbers of people, few of whom are affected strongly enough to voice concern.[2] In these and other circumstances, decision makers are unlikely to possess strong personal preferences nor are they likely to receive strong signals from the environment. The existence of wide agreement on broad social goals such as economic growth, wilderness preservation, or improvement in the situation of the poor, does not help much in dealing with specific problems as they arise. Therefore, especially for choices which involve unfamiliar factors and thus are of a nonroutine sort, considered preferences will be confined to choices that bear on subordinate issues rather than on the larger ones.

Second, the nature of the problem may be obscure. The occasion for believing that "something should be done" may be the emergence of a symptom (e.g., an unexpected increase in a price index), an event (e.g., the failure of New York City to sell a bond issue), a new technological possibility (e.g., a report that asserts that supersonic transportation is technically feasible), a proposal (e.g., for building a dam on the Delaware River). The event that brings the problem to the top of the action agenda focuses attention but does not define it well enough for sensible decision. Instead, events generate a search for information about the problem and possible alternative courses of action and objectives. The ends to be sought and the means that might be employed are a joint product of the inquiry undertaken.

Third, available "solutions" are unpersuasive. They do not seem to deal with the problem, however it is perceived; they seem infeasible, or at least too costly. And even if some appear at first glance to be adequate, there may be large uncertainties about how well they would really work.

Fourth, policy decisions are, in general, not made by single individuals acting over time. Nor are they usually made by a group of people acting jointly in committee. They are usually shaped instead by the interaction over time and space of individuals with different attitudes, skills, information, and influence. Most of the participants operate in organizations with missions that inevitably filter data and shape the policy alternatives generated. Organizational biases often interfere with the process of consensus building. But agreement on the consequences of choices and values is not needed for action and therefore normally does not occur. All that is essential is agreement on the next step.

In Position A, therefore, a decision maker must develop or construct his preferences and the alternatives for meeting them. He does this by using methods that have worked in the past for himself or for others in similar situations; or he defines away the problem by declaring that it falls within existing policy; or he uses intuition; or he calls on expert advice; or he fools around with data in different ways and tries out different objectives and alternatives. To those in Position A, *the contribution of policy analysis is essentially heuristic: to provide a conceptual framework (or several) for relating means to ends, for thinking about ends, for identifying the existing technical alternatives, and for inventing new ones.*

The analysis of Tocks provides examples of a heuristic process at work. Although most of the participants may have begun with a notion—indeed, a conviction—about what was the "right" thing to do, the process of investigation did turn up some new things: alternative means of providing various degrees of flood control, clarification about the different kinds of recreation that would be provided by dam and no-dam alternatives, ideas about other sources of water for New Jersey. Quite a few forecasts were made, about water quality and population growth for instance. I do not know what the total effect of these estimates and alternatives was on the analyst participants or on the governors who have recently made some decisions on Tocks, but it seems to me more plausible to conjecture that many of the participants went through a learning process than that they merely generated—or received—inputs for some predetermined objective functions.

In short, for many participants the analytic process will contribute to beliefs about facts and relationships and will help in the construction of value preferences. The phrase "construction of value preferences" is deliberately chosen. This reflects the view that preferences are generally built through experience and through learning about facts, about relationships, and about consequences. It is not that values are latent and only need to be "discovered" or "revealed." There is a potentially infinite number of values; they are not equally useful or valid, and part of the task of analysis is to develop ones that seem especially "right" and useful and that might become widely shared. Because value preferences are formed through a process of choice in specific cultural and institutional settings, and because, as Laurence Tribe observes, avoidance of dissonance causes us to prefer what we have chosen, the factors that influence our choices get imbedded in our values. Those that are fuzzy, fragile, not immediately useful, are likely to be excluded and therefore are not built into the value system that we are constantly constructing and reconstructing.

III

Another decision maker is in a different position (let us call it Position B)—a position he perceives as less ambiguous than Position A because he has well defined objectives. (Other people may believe that his goals *should* be different ones.) He is looking for better alternatives, perhaps even for an optimum. He may engage in a vigorous search for alternatives. He will probably look for it by searching in the neighborhood of other alternatives that have worked well for him in the past or seem to have worked well for others in similar situations.[3] If this isn't sufficient, he may have to do more serious searching over a wider domain. He may put his analytic staff to work inventing broadly different alternatives. Here also is to be found the policy maker who has a "solution" and is looking for a problem (e.g., a bureau head looking for business for his agency). He may put his analytic staff to work identifying unmet or inventing hitherto unknown needs of whose importance other decision makers might be persuaded, along with the desirability of his solution.

Recently, a search process was engaged in by the National Aeronautics and Space Administration as it neared the end of the Apollo Program. The "solution" was employment for the existing manned space program. An extensive search was undertaken for jobs to be done through that program within budgets that might be available. During the course of these analyses, a good deal of work and a certain amount of ingenuity was applied to the problem of defining tasks that could be done by men in space and in arguing that the benefits would exceed the costs. The Corps of Engineers' advocacy of the Tocks Island Dam on the Delaware River looks like a similar case. Much of the behavior of government agencies is similarly motivated. Agencies have product lines or specialized services that they promote in the political marketplace, and they sometimes use the tools of analysis both to help improve their products and to help sell them.

Often, nongovernmental (although not necessarily nonpartisan) analysts are also to be found in Position B. The analyst who "knows" it is a terrible mistake to build a large dam at Tocks *has* his values. What analysis can do for him is to marshall the evidence on the costs and benefits of proceeding with this project, to spell out consequences that may have been overlooked, and—most important—to provide a framework for proposing alternatives (e.g., different ways of providing flood control on the Delaware flood plain).

A person in Position B is more likely than one in A to perceive analysis as useful, not only heuristically, but also in providing what might be called a "decision rule" for choosing a preferred alternative. However, the decision rule use of analysis requires that outputs be well defined, quantifiable, and preferably reducible to the same currency as costs, or at least that enough of them can be so expressed to make it a useful exercise. This is unlikely to be possible in the case of larger and more complex policy issues that arise and more likely to work on repetitive and narrower questions. In both, however, there is a significant role for design and invention. Indeed, it is in circumstances in which commitments to policies and programs are strongest, where conflicts with other explicit public purposes or with poorly represented values are greatest, that inventive ingenuity is most valuable. The invention of new possibilities may help shift policy choices away from perhaps intractable zero-sum choices to nonzero-sum choices—from choices where what some people gain others lose to those where there are gains for all.

Policy analysis, as described so far, would seem to be an unalloyed good. This is not universally believed to be so. Practical men sometimes say that it is too complicated to be useful, that analysts are more interested in exercising their analytical skills or merely adding to the sum of human knowledge than in helping to solve policy problems. These practical men are not always wrong. Other, more fundamental, criticisms of policy analysis, expressed most eloquently by Laurence Tribe,[4] are that policy analysis: (1) concentrates on tangible, quantifiable factors and ignores or depreciates the importance of intangible, unquantifiable ones; (2) leaves out of consideration altogether certain "fragile" values—e.g., ecological or esthetic concerns; (3) focuses on results and, in its search for common measures, ignores both the processes by which preferences and decisions are formed and significant qualitative differences among outcomes; (4) tends to operate within limits set by the interests and values of the clients; (5) in the effort to be objective, employs deceptively neutral and detached language in dealing with intensely moral issues; (6) artificially separates facts from values; and (7) tends to overlook distributional objectives in favor of efficiency objectives.

These criticisms clearly apply to bad analysis—i.e., to analysis that fails to possess the characteristics listed earlier. And much analysis is bad. But they excessively depreciate the value of analysis that is incomplete or partisan. For example, as Allen Carlin and Alain Enthoven have argued in our discussions, even a narrow analysis can sometimes make a powerful case that an unwise proposal is in fact a bad one (e.g., that a supersonic transport will not be economically viable). Such analyses are useful. The criticisms listed above do have validity, but they are most appropriately cited against the claim that analysis provides a rule for choice. Their relevance to the heuristic function, which I argue is the principal one for analysis, is less clear.

There does not seem to be serious disagreement about some of the characteristics of the kind of analysis that is needed. Proper analysis as proposed by Laurence Tribe, for example, would point

... in the general direction of a subtler, more holistic, and more complex style of problem solving, undoubtedly involving several iterations between problem formulation and problem solution and relying at each stage on the careful articulation of a wide range of interrelated values and constraints through the development of several distinct "perspectives" on a given problem, each couched in an idiom true to its internal structure rather than translated into some "common denominator."[5]

I would add: "and which seeks to develop new action possibilities and new objectives that might be sought." But I think it should be recognized that a pluralistic political system in which the participants use the techniques of policy analysis—narrow and partisan though they may be—can approximate the holistic style Tribe advocates, although I would not claim that the observation of such an analytic marketplace at work is an everyday experience.

This view of analysis is, I believe, a helpful one in relation to our central concern—namely, the neglect of fragile, fuzzy, currently nonoperational values. It has often been observed that we have invented institutional means for the protection or representation of values that are systematically neglected. We have done this by passing laws to protect the rights of minorities or to require an environmental impact statement for projects; we have done it by setting up government agencies to promote arms control and disarmament or environmental protection or the interests of the poor. But the threshold for the passage of laws and the creation of new agencies is not low. It is fair to ask what analysis can do to help to improve on this situation.

One way is to study complex environmental phenomena and to try to identify unexpected consequences of private or public actions. Another is to explore some of the long-run consequences of the neglect of certain values, and to stimulate the collection of illustrative data. Many people who do not think much from day to day about the decline in the number of whales or black-footed ferrets, when presented with data and analyses that record their decline and predict their extinction, may come to feel that this is a problem about which something must be done. And because the political process sometimes leads politicians to search actively for causes that have not been preempted by others, it is sometimes possible to connect neglected interests with those looking for issues to promote. This is a kind of lottery and it is also a kind of market test; those values that cannot command the votes or capture the imagination of politicians or are not protected by constitutional guarantee will not do well. It is a challenge to analysts not only to do the kind of substantive analysis they have traditionally done, but also to devise ways of describing fuzzy or neglected phenomena and to invent ways of injecting them into decision processes.

IV

One of the most urgent needs, in my view, is achieving much deeper knowledge of the nature of governmental processes than the conventional learning provides. Policy outcomes are strongly influenced by the missions and structure of Executive branch agencies and congressional committees. Initially structured by law, they have evolved through time and experience, and have been constrained by technology and influenced by interest groups. It is not much of an oversimplification to assert that each major bureaucratic entity—bureau, agency, department—comes to have a special character which dominates its behavior. For example, the Corps of Engineers and the Bureau of Reclamation do not have as objectives the avoidance of flood damage, improvements in the efficiency of transportation, or increases in electric power production, but rather the carrying out of large-scale construction projects which contribute to these ends. An alternative, such as use of the price mechanism to help achieve those goals, is not generally within the policy space available to these agencies.

This kind of constraint on instrumentalities might be thought to be less in the case of departments with broader missions, such as Justice, Defense, or State. To some extent this is so, but these departments consist of aggregations of organizational entities, each with its own limited perspective, and the behavior of the collective largely reflects the behavior of the constituent parts. Congress usually proceeds in a similarly constrained manner through the action of committees that occupy well marked out turfs. And members of these committees are often moved by concerns even more parochial than those of the agencies they oversee. How a problem is treated is therefore largely determined by which agency gets the action. How differently might the Tocks problem have been viewed if it had been initially defined principally as a recreation problem and preempted by the National Park Service as a Delaware Water Gap National Recreation Area project?

Both the definition of the problem and the range of admissible solutions differs according to which agency comes to have principal responsibility. Moreover, the probability is low in most arenas that the dominant problem definition will be seriously challenged by other bureaucratic interests. The boundaries of territorial rights are well known and usually observed. Struggles do occur from time to time, but they are costly; and a taste for the quiet life leads agency heads usually to prefer private horse trades to public fights. Nongovernmental interests are much more likely to mount overt challenges, but they are usually less well entrenched legally, they are less well armed with analytic resources, and they often have less staying power.

Organizational behavior can also plausibly be associated with many of the observed shortcomings in analysis discussed earlier. Does the frequently observed failure of analyses to use choice criteria sensitively or to give adequate weight to qualitative factors reflect only or mainly the limitations of analytic techniques or of the analyst's values or training? I think not. One must also look to the organizational setting in which analysis is done. If the performance of bureaucrats and analysts is judged on the basis of certain numbers (and it often is), then these performance measures have a powerful incentive on behavior. It should not be surprising that importance is attached in analyses to dollar measures such as sales of timber from national forests or physical measures such as recreation-days if these criteria are of great importance within the organizations that dominate many environmental decisions.

Observing the powerful role of organizational interests suggests an area of inquiry that is almost totally neglected by policy analysts, whose work has been largely focused on improvements in the tools of analysis or on applying these tools to substantive problems. This is the systematic study of the behavior of the principal institutions that shape public choices, their perception of their central purposes, the rules by which they operate, their internal systems of incentives and controls, and the means by which they seek to influence their external environment. The resulting hypotheses about their behavior could then be used to predict the alternatives that might be suggested when policy issues arise and to predict outcomes of policy decisions.

Perhaps the greatest current need, a need that organization theorists and students of bureaucratic functioning have only begun to meet, is the systematic study of policy implementation. We often refer to "a policy decision" as the end point of the analytic process. But more often than not "a policy decision" is but one move in a continuing decision process. An authoritative decision or cluster of decisions (e.g., the passage of a law and the appropriation of funds) may be necessary for *something* to happen, but it is usually not enough to determine *what* will happen. The realm of administrative discretion is usually large. This is as it should be, for the alternative of trying to legislate ever more detailed means as well as broader purposes would be worse.

Many important choices are made during implementation; but neither the choices made by people at a low level in the organizational hierarchy nor the consequences of their actions may be obvious to what is somewhat inaccurately called the "policy levels." And sometimes the "policy levels" have little incentive to find out what is actually going on. In short, analysts who do not understand the salient characteristics of the bureaucratic system responsible for carrying out any given policy alternative cannot predict with much confidence what actually would happen if that alternative were adopted. With the kind of organizational knowledge that only a few now possess and that none possesses as fully or deeply as desirable, analysts could help to design alternatives which would have a higher probability of achieving the predicted or desired results. They would also be in a position to propose organizational changes that would alter the incentives and therefore the behavior of the dominant institutions.

In sum, the study of implementation behavior in organizations is the study of instrumentalities for achieving social purposes. And those who believe that important social values are neglected need to exercise ingenuity in devising mechanisms for the representation of these values. If the Sierra Club, the Friends of the Earth, and the Environmental Protection Agency did not exist they would probably be invented. But many more inventions are still needed to promote values of the sort these groups embody. The encouragement and support of the type of policy analysis they perform—perhaps it should be called meta-policy analysis—should be high on the agenda of any national environmental research program.

V

It is important to consider what components a fully developed system of analytic organizations that was equipped to carry out a broad spectrum of policy-related studies on environmental questions would include. The following array would represent a well-developed capacity for handling the analytic aspects of environmental problems:

1. In-house government staffs to do staff analyses, to make use of the policy analysis of external researchers, and to stimulate and sponsor new outside research.

2. Laboratories—governmental and nongovernmental—working in a wide range of technical areas.
3. A for-profit analytical services industry.
4. Manufacturing industry that produces prototypes and production items.
5. Academic research on a wide range of basic and applied areas.
6. Broad, interdisciplinary, long term research programs carried out in one or more large nongovernmental research institutions.
7. Small special purpose research institutes that concentrate on specific problem areas such as wildlife preservation.
8. State or regional analytic organizations to do project analyses in depth.
9. An environmental research agency responsible for identifying and funding important gaps in the research and analysis carried out by the mission agencies.
10. A set of membership organizations, trade associations, and consumer oriented groups that engage in advocacy analysis.
11. One or more journals that regularly review major policy analysis on environmental questions.

Parts of this environmental-industrial-governmental complex already exist, and the supply of trained analysts is increasing. A recent development of potential importance is a Ford Foundation grant to Resources For the Future for a broader program of work that could permit RFF to become a major contributor to policy related analysis in the environmental field. If so, it would fill one of the more obvious institutional gaps—the absence of a broad environmental research institute of the type proposed a few years ago. The concept then was to create a private organization that contracted with government agencies to do both policy oriented research and related background studies. It was also to have had a significant amount of relatively unconstrained nongovernmental funding. Much of its work was to have been organized on a long term programmatic basis; but some would have been on near-term policy issues. The institute's program would have included systematic analysis of the generalized waste products problem, the theory of exploitation of depletable resources, land use problems, the technologies of pollution control, the use of market vs. nonmarket instruments, the study of behavior of organizations which affect the environment, and—not least—mechanisms by which environmental values might be effectively incorporated into public sector decision processes. This model is close to that of Rand; the major difference is that the proposed institute would have had a greater proportion of nongovernmental foundation funding. The central feature of this model is that both work on policy issues *and* broad system studies would be carried out within one organization. Perhaps now RFF will become that organization.

The proposal for a gap-filling environmental research agency is based on the observation that the bureaucratic constraints of operational mission agencies inevitably cause important research and analytic questions to be overlooked. This institution's task would, therefore, be to sponsor work on important neglected topics. Its work would be done largely on contract with outside organizations because the areas of need would shift substantially over time. The institutional model here is ARPA, the Advanced Research Projects Agency of the Defense Department.

Small special purpose research organizations would have the advantages of the concentration, technical competency, and dedication that can be achieved through a focused effort in a specific area. Some possible missions for such special purpose institutes might be wildlife preservation, development of recreational opportunities, studies of land use (e.g., a Land Use Center has been established recently by the Urban Institute), wetlands preservation, and energy and materials conservation. These organizations could serve as sources of information by providing inputs to other project analyses, but most important, they would generate ideas to further their own missions.

State and regional analytic organizations could provide resources for project analyses and act as a counterbalance to the federal agencies which dominate project analyses now. These regional institutes might be financed by both federal and state funds.

There is, in addition, the important task of developing and maintaining professional standards, exposing shoddy work, and arranging to have analyses done from different perspectives meet head-on. The academic journals do this in scholarly fields. But this mechanism has not worked well in the field of policy analysis because the range of substantive areas covered is large, publication channels are varied, and the standards of performance are ill-defined. Disciplined, thorough review of major pieces of policy analysis is rare. A recent effort to review standards in one area suggests a reason why: the inquiry undertaken several years ago by the Operations Research Society of America (ORSA) into the analytic aspects of testimony on antiballistic missiles led to a useful review of some of the calculations that were used to support widely varying policy positions taken on the ABM.[6] But it also raised controversial questions about the proper role of professional organizations in purporting to "police" the analytic and advisory activities of their own, and related, professionals. Therefore, groups like ORSA are unlikely to make this kind of inquiry a regular activity, and other means for carrying out careful review of major analytic and advisory products are needed. Fortunately, a new journal being started at the University of California (Berkeley) Graduate School of Public Policy has this as one of its stated purposes.

VI

Finally, it can hardly be doubted that environmental problems are among those most in need of, and ultimately susceptible to, systematic analysis. Many of them are enormously complex—so much so that counterintuitive consequences are often to be expected. After all, one of the basic concepts in ecology is the notion of the "system," with its complex interrelations and with the possibility of remote repercussions from current decisions. This is a field of endeavor that requires an enormously wide range of research: basic scientific investigation, methodological innovations, the forecasting of trends, specific policy studies, the investigation of decision processes, and devising means for bringing together the knowledge and skills of experts from many fields in close and continuing working arrangements. If this can be done, it is likely to have a very high payoff indeed.

But in the end, the work of the analyst must be supplemented by that of the artist, poet, and novelist. Policy analysis has its virtues, but the large changes in society are brought about through processes of which it now knows little—processes about which it can hope to learn a little more.

NOTES

1. For a similar view of preference formation and the role of analysis see James G. March, "The Technology of Foolishness," in *Civiløkonomen*, Copenhagen, vol. 18, May 1971, pp. 4–12. For an earlier statement see Albert Wohlstetter, "Analysis and Design Conflict Systems," in *Analysis for Military Decision*, ed. by E.S. Quade (Santa Monica, Calif.: Rand Corp., 1964). This essay was based on lectures given at Rand in 1954–55.

2. See the article by Mancur Olson in *Evaluation*, vol. 1, no. 2, 1973.

3. John D. Steinbruner, *The Cybernetic Theory of Decision—New Dimensions of Political Analysis* (Princeton, N.J.: Princeton University Press, 1974).

4. See Laurence Tribe, "Policy Science: Analysis or Ideology?" *Philosophy and Public Affairs* (Fall 1972): 66–110.

5. *Ibid.*, p. 107.

6. "Guidelines for the Practice of Operations Research," *Operations Research* 19, (5), (September 1971): 1123–1258.

Chapter Seven

An Afterword:
Humane Values and
Environmental Decisions

Robert Dorfman

The Academy project on the incorporation of humane values into environmental decision making extended from December 1971 to September 1974. In the course of its long life at least three dozen people participated and contributed. The reports, drafts, and supporting documents that it generated fill a large filing drawer.

This concluding essay was planned to be a final conspectus of the project. But that is not practicable. None of the participants in a large project can pronounce definitive judgment on the works of the others. Any participant can report only what he has learned from his own work and from studying the work of his colleagues. The other participants have spoken for themselves in the preceding essays and in a companion volume. Here I shall describe where I now stand in light of all this work; the upshot as viewed by any of the others would surely be different in many respects. Since this essay is largely a record of my own learning experience, I shall occasionally lapse into the first person singular.

"An economist," according to Oscar Wilde, "is a man who knows the price of everything and the value of nothing." To which a well-trained economist would respond, "But, Mr. Wilde, prices *are* values." There is much justice in this riposte, and it can be documented by a long shelf of weighty volumes that purport to prove it. But despite the ponderous evidence, Mr. Wilde could win this fictitious debate if he had the patience to tackle the technicalities and ferret out the assumptions on which the economist's "proofs" rest. Two assumptions are especially suspect. First, that the value of anything that a consumer purchases is measured by what he is willing to pay for it. An effete snob such as Oscar Wilde could never concede that the ordinary man-in-the-street is a competent judge of the values of the things that he buys or does. In fact, you don't have to be a notorious effete snob to harbor some doubts about this assumption. The second questionable assumption is that the consequences of all transactions are reflected fully in market-determined prices. This is so far from being the case that it would not be too bad a summary to say that all environmental problems result from transactions in which market prices are either absent or are seriously distorted because of special circumstances.

Nowadays, at any rate, even economists and people of similar ilk concede that they know far more about prices than about values. The study that this essay concludes was motivated by the accompanying recognition that values rather than prices should be the decisive concern in environmental decisions. But how can values be ascertained, how articulated, and how made to shape the decision-making process? Those are the questions that have dominated the project from its inception. None has been resolved, but all have been explored and, to some degree, clarified.

EMERGENCE OF THE PROBLEM

Environmental decisions are only leading members of a large class of social decisions, namely, social decisions about the use of resources in circumstances where the consequences are deemed too important to the social welfare to be entrusted to purely private use and allocation. Such decisions are far from novel, even in the United States where there is a strong tradition of reliance on individualism and individual judgment. The construction of the transcontinental railroad in the 1860s, with the vigorous sponsorship of the federal government, probably had as profound an effect on our environment as any other social decision in our history. The construction of the Erie Canal 40 years previously had similar effects.

The environmental impacts of these and similar decisions were not inadvertent; on the contrary, the conscious intent was to "open up the West." No one, however, thought of filing or demanding an environmental impact statement. It was simply taken for granted that the wilderness was so abundant that it could be invaded without heed or restraint. Technically speaking, undisturbed wilderness was regarded as a free good; the Homestead Act of the 1870s made it legally a free good. Under this act and related policies, vast tracts were given away for the asking, until by the end of the century the wilderness had been devoured except where there was insufficient water or insufficient level ground to make cultivation worthwhile.

This spirit of unconstrained conquest of nature continued unabated until at least the 1930s. The great flood control, irrigation, and hydroelectric projects of that epoch were constructed under the provisions of the Flood Control Act of 1936, which laid down the standard that the total benefits anticipated from any project had to exceed its costs. The words "benefits" and "costs" were not carefully defined in that Act, or for many years later, but in the early projects developed under the act they were given a businesslike, dollars-and-cents interpretation, apparently with full congressional approval. If a huge project for developing the environment appeared to be a profitable business proposition, it met the standard and could be built.

All along, of course, opposing, cautionary voices were raised, reaching a climax in the conservation movement at the turn of the century. Important local victories were won by the conservationists. Most strikingly, Yellowstone National Park was established in 1872, soon followed by Yosemite and a number of others, thus establishing the precedent for reserving for public use natural areas of unique beauty or significance. But the main emphasis was to turn the natural wealth of the continent to commercially profitable uses. Meanwhile the balance of resources was shifting. The formerly free goods were becoming scarce as population increased, per capita wealth grew, and the remaining undisturbed area shrank. The shift was largely unnoticed, but there were portents—particularly the cut-over forests of northern Michigan, the Mississippi floods, and the fearful storms in the "dust bowl" that replaced an abundant prairie. In the 1930s, while exploitation was still the major theme, attention to conservation began to grow. The frontier was long since gone, and the consequences of past depredations were becoming visible.

World War II was a dividing line. From it there emerged a wealthy and urbanized nation. What that entailed for the environment soon became evident, most dramatically in Los Angeles but also along the Ohio and other urbanized rivers. Not that there was any abrupt change in public attitudes. Previously ugliness and dirt had been accepted and even hailed as the inevitable signs of urban life, and they were tolerated unquestioningly except when they posed clearly perceived threats to life and health. But in the 1950s they were seen to be conditions that man had made and that, in a wealthy country, he could doubtless unmake. Thus Pittsburgh, which had long been accustomed to living under a blanket of soot, banned the use of bituminous coal in the built-up area, and many other cities followed.

In Los Angeles, after the smog had grown from an occasional inconvenience to a persistent insult, it was diagnosed and vigorously combatted. Along the Ohio and other rivers the improvement of water quality became more urgent than providing still more water for still more agriculture and industry. The "free" goods were no longer free. Furthermore, private initiative could not be counted on to conserve them. Public environmental policies and programs were clearly seen as necessary by the 1960s, and probes began to be taken in the Air Quality Act and the Water Pollution Control Act in the middle of the decade.

By the time public attention turned from commercial exploitation of the environment to preserving its quality, benefit-cost analysis, formally introduced for water projects in 1936, had become entrenched as the dominant conceptual framework for designing and appraising public projects of almost every conceivable sort, both in the United States and abroad. This framework, it should be remembered, was developed under the older regime, and amounted essentially to balancing the commercial value of the results of a project against the comparable value of the resources it absorbed. There was no place in it for environmental quality, esthetics, or public health and welfare—a defect that caused increasing discomfort as these aspects of projects became increasingly important and came increasingly to dominate public awareness. But benefit-cost analysis remained very nearly the only recognized method of project analysis and justification.

The stress created by this circumstance has been well described by Arthur Maass:

> In other words, the objective functions of most government programs are complex; yet benefit-cost analysis has been adapted to only a single objective—economic efficiency. ... Professor Hubert Marshall recently recited the evidences of chronic overestimation (of benefits) in a major address before the Western Resources Conference at Fort Collins. The principal cause of such benefit "over-estimation" is, I believe, the unreal restrictions placed on the analysis of projects by the unreal but virtual standard that the relationship of efficiency benefits to efficiency costs is the indicator of a project's worth, when in fact the project is conceived and planned for objectives in addition to efficiency. In such an incongruous circumstance one might expect project planners to use a broad definition of efficiency benefits. The critics, either not understanding or unsympathetic to the planners' plight, have judged them by a more rigorous definition of efficiency.[1]

Thus, though the words of benefit-cost analysis remained the same, their contents changed, for the most part insensibly and without explicit avowal. Commercial values became imputed values. The Corps of Engineers, the very citadel of benefit-cost analysis, received legal authority to include "recreation benefits" in its project evaluations, and soon recreation benefits became the decisive ingredient of many projects. But the new "intangibles" did not sit very well side-by-side with the old hard estimates of increases in crop value and value of electric power. It was a case of trying to pour new wine into an old bottle with a very narrow neck, a messy job at best.

Now, no stream has a single source. We have traced how public attitudes towards the environment changed as population and wealth grew and less readily reversible inroads upon the environment became more apparent. We have also seen how the methods of public decision making at the formal level, developed in accordance with older attitudes, were so well entrenched that they persisted, although they were seen to be increasingly inappropriate to the new demands placed on them. At the same time, other developments were taking place, which interacted with the stream we have just reviewed.

One of these developments was a body of techniques variously called operations research, systems analysis, management science, and, most recently, policy analysis. They became prominent during World War II as an adjunct to military decision making. But, of course, the application of scientific formulations to practical decisions, which is the heart of all these techniques, is very old. Machievelli and DaVinci were distinguished practitioners. Archimedes made fundamental contributions. Aristotle was a consultant to the King of Macedon; he may have been the progenitor. Nevertheless, as a distinct, self-conscious, distinguishable skill and profession, policy analysis is barely thirty years old. Those are the thirty years that concern us here. They can be characterized as thirty years of fading innocence.

Thirty years ago it all seemed to those of us who practiced it very simple in principle, though intriguingly intricate in technique. The task of policy analysis could be stated in four words: *Maximization subject to constraint.* The Decision Maker (a fictitious character about whom more will later be said) knew what he wanted and turned to his consultant to find the best way to achieve it. The consultant, for his part, had no concern with objectives or ends; his department was techniques, or means. Give him an objective—any old objective—and he deployed a large armament of analytic methods—statistics, simulations, queuing theory, mathematical programming, game theory, optimal control theory, and much more—to discover how the objective could be attained in the highest possible degree (though only in a discounted expected value sense in a dynamic, stochastic world).

From the very beginning, in spite of some spectacular achievements, the clients were frequently dissatisfied, and the practitioners correspondingly frustrated. All too often, the client ignored the elegant appendices, looked at the recommendations, shook his head, and said, "That won't do at all. That isn't what I had in mind at all. You have left out the crucial considerations." There was no point in remonstrating, in saying, "But I did maximize the objective function you told me about." The analyst had solved the wrong problem, and that's all there was to it.

A growing profession spawns textbooks, and by the time the first texts were out this pitfall had been recognized. The texts of, say, twenty years ago were not complete without a homily on the importance of choosing the objective function carefully, followed by an example or two of the disasters caused by inattention to this advice. The tidy separation of means from ends was still not questioned overtly—but it was beginning to be smudged. At the same time, a different set of difficulties was arising that reinforced concern about the role of objectives in policy analysis. While still accepting the mandate to maximize the value of a preassigned objective function, analysts were becoming aware that it was frequently hard for anyone to ascertain just what the objective function was or ought to be.

Perhaps the first professional group to encounter this problem on a large and unsettling scale were the federal benefit-cost analysts, whom we have already mentioned. They began their work under the aegis of the Flood Control Act of 1936. The early great dams planned in the West under this act were designed primarily for irrigation water, hydroelectric power, and flood protection. So they produced or protected commodities with fairly readily ascertainable market values, and their benefits were readily estimated, aside from some technical problems with discount rates, double-counting, and market imperfections. But when the same apparatus was turned on projects designed for more subtle purposes, the original clarity faded. "Intangibles" and "incommensurables" began to play large parts.

It was at this stage that the "cost effectiveness" mode of analysis was introduced. Cost effectiveness analyses take as their points of departure specified levels of attainment of various beneficial results—for example, specified reductions in atmospheric sulphur oxides, or specified amounts of outdoor recreational opportunities—and then inquire whether a given proposed plan is the cheapest way to attain them. If it is, that plan is said to be cost effective. This approach is a substantial retreat from the older pretensions of policy analysis or of benefit-cost analysis. It abjures the attempt to compare the worthwhileness of the gains with the amount of the costs. It cannot be used to compare plans with different patterns of gains, for example, plans that preserve larger areas of natural ecological systems with those that provide more extensive recreational areas. In general, both its advantage and its drawback are that it evades the task of formulating an inclusive objective function in which different consequences are weighed against each other. Instead, it merely implements the aspiration that whatever is to be done—worthwhile or not—be done as cheaply as possible. It has its place when specific targets to be attained are prescribed. But it is of no help in prescribing the targets.

"Multiobjective planning" is a more recent proposal for filling this gap, but it too is a way of shifting responsibility rather than of solving the problem. Multiobjective planning starts with the recognition that any project has numerous effects and consequences and that, while each individual effect may be numerically measurable in its own units, there is likely to be no common objective unit by which the magnitudes of the different effects can be compared and evaluated. It therefore recommends planning a project so that its performance cannot be improved in any identified respect without impairment in other respects—and there it stops. Final judgment has to be made by comparing variant projects that excel each other in different directions (one may be cheapest, another may disturb the environment the least, a third may provide most protection against droughts), and somehow deciding which, if any, to adopt. The method makes a point of not articulating how this final judgment is to be made and, indeed, rests with the belief that such articulation is impossible. It is, therefore, the ultimate development in emphasizing the distinction between designating goals or values and devising means for attaining them.

Such has been the evolution of increasing sophistication in policy analysis. At first it was assumed that whenever a policy problem arose, the ends desired were perfectly obvious, and that the only difficulty was to devise the means for attaining those well-established ends. At that stage, the systems and policy analysts were exceedingly proud of the prowess with which they wielded powerful new developments in applied mathematics and computing machinery. The assumption proved to be false: goals were even more subtle and elusive than means. What was the use of powerful maximizing techniques if no one could tell what was to be maximized? There followed an increasing preoccupation with goals—at first an attempt to define them, and later an explicit decision to leave them to someone else, the "Decision Maker."

That evolution in the technique of policy analysis has not occurred in a vacuum. At least in part, it is a reflection of some tendencies in the general culture, tendencies that may have been stimulated as a reaction against the coolly manipulative, value-free pretensions of the policy analysts. Thus, the public fears the think tanks with their big computers. The public has recognized at least as soon as the professionals that objectives cannot safely be left out of the analysis. And the public is fearful of a government and society that takes advice from model builders as soulless as the analysts professed to be.

I do not want to be taken to suggest that the current resurgence of romanticism can be attributed in any significant part to the failings of the policy analysts. What is significant is that there is such a reaction against the dominant rationalistic, skeptical, pragmatic philosophy, and that it has focused on computer-aided policy analysis as its symbol of science-gone-wild. This reaction has invaded even economics, which, perhaps, has the most firmly established tradition of separating ends from means, purposes from possibilities, demands from supplies. For some time now there has been a strong attack on the deep-seated assumption that an economy has done its job when it has satisfied the individual demands of its individual consumers. The animus has much in common with the dissatisfaction that I recounted with policy analysis. Consumers' demands are felt to be insufficiently enduring, well established, or independent of the economic process itself to serve as a firm criterion for economic performance. Consumers' demands and tastes are, to use one of the kinder phrases in vogue, simply the result of social conditioning, and besides give insufficient weight to communal goals and aspirations.

So, from a number of angles of vision, the established methods of analysing decisions have been found wanting, and always in very much the same respects. No one challenges seriously that, in a slavish way, the new analytic techniques have vastly amplified our ability to design and appraise projects in the light of given objectives. The challenge is, rather, that our skill in attaining objectives has outrun our skill in determining or even articulating them.

One might say that science has done its work but philosophy has not, and the gap has become so egregious that even the scientists have noticed. The fault, in my view at least, is not with the scientists. They started out courageously showing how they could help society attain simple—even simplistic—goals, such as maximizing the commercial value produced by the use of natural resources. When it was clear that society's goals were more subtle and complicated than that, they called for a more adequate statement of the goals to be attained. But no one answered. Then they set about trying to discover the goals for themselves by the only method they know: empirical analysis. That approach has not proved fruitful, because scientific analysis presupposes a coherent, internally consistent universe to be studied, and those do not seem to be qualities that can be asserted of social goals. The scientists are still at it, trying to discover by scientific observation what people's goals really are so that the tools of policy analysis can be used uncritically to implement them. The most potent work currently seems to be that of the decision analysis school, as exemplified by Howard Raiffa, Ralph Keeney, and their followers.

But we have to question the entire concept of an immutable set of goals to be accepted uncritically by the policy analyst. We have to contemplate the possibility—often reiterated in the folk tale of the man who had three wishes—that, if we could get what we think we want, we wouldn't like it. Why? Why is it that fulfillment is a mirage, that every attainment reveals its own inadequacy, that there is always another hill to climb, that, in particular, when we have conquered the continent we realized that that was not what we wanted at all? Is it because we are insatiably greedy? On the contrary, we only think we are. "Ah cannot we as well as cocks and lyons jocund be, after such pleasures?" We cannot, because we are not cocks and lyons.

The philosophers knew all along that pleasures attained cloy rather than satisfy. How is the policy analyst to get even that degree of philosophic sophistication and folk wisdom into the objective function he uses in his analysis? He must do that or else he is condemned to the endless, tedious wheel of *samsara*—that is, to the service of perpetually unsatisfying goals. Those words are not a sermon, but a diagnosis of the current state of dissatisfaction. The policy analysts are dissatisfied because they do not want the responsibility of defining the objectives of the policies they study. The clients are dissatisfied because they do not accept the goals that the analysts ascribe to them. Public observers are dissatisfied because they do not trust the cold-blooded analysts to set their society's objectives.

AN OLD DIAGNOSIS

It is not often that one of the tritest cliches of all philosophies and religions finds scientific application, but this appears to be an instance when it might: If man does not live by bread alone, then hard-headed policy analyses that concentrate attention on wheat yields are bound to be unsatisfying. Something is clearly left out, something we can call humane or higher values. But the objective, scientific approach does not know how to either detect humane and moral values or measure them, and is strongly inhibited against imposing them.

When all the technical trappings are stripped away, modern policy analysis is seen to be essentially an application of old-fashioned utilitarianism.[2] Almost from its inception, utilitarianism was reproached for being crassly materialistic, which is just the failing that its current applications have been unable to avoid despite increasing qualms. But materialism is not inherent in utilitarian philosophy, nor considering the austere orientations of its advocates, is the charge even plausible. John Stuart Mill, undoubtedly the preeminent exponent of utilitarianism, was well aware that social policy must be informed by higher moral purpose. He wrote:

> We may consider, then, as one criterion of the goodness of a government, the degree in which it tends to increase the sum of good qualities in the governed, collectively and individually; since besides that their well-being is the sole object of government, their good qualities supply the moving force which works the machinery.[3]

This is a far cry from benefit-cost analysis or from the stated goals of any of the prevalent modes of policy analysis. Mill's dictum recognizes that public decisions should address themselves to moral consequences, which, as we were led to suspect above, is the missing ingredient in current policy analysis.

It will not do to minimize the difficulty of accepting Mill's criterion. Such a Victorian doctrine does not comport well with computing machines. It poses questions that no scientifically indoctrinated analyst cares to answer. What are "good qualities," and what "tends to increase their sum," if indeed they have a sum? Mill and his contemporary followers haven't answered those questions, but they have raised them, which is a good deal. I do not believe that those questions can be answered definitively, now or ever; but neither can they be ignored. The progress that I see in our project is that it points the way to living honestly with those forever open questions.

TRIBE'S PRESCRIPTION

Mill's dictum, then, is that an important consideration in evaluating a public undertaking, environmental or otherwise, is "the degree in which it tends to increase the sum of good qualities in the governed." At first blush this may seem excessively high-minded and impractical, but our review of the current predicament of policy analysis indicates that policy analysis has to take account of just such high-minded purposes if it is to escape from its current frustrations. If this be so, we have to find a way to bring a concern for good qualities into the decision process—in spite of the fact that no one can be trusted to decide what would be good qualities for someone else to have. As I understand it, this is just what Laurence Tribe's proposal for a synthesis through "process" amounts to. (That proposal is described in some detail in his essay in this volume.)

Let us call Tribe's proposal "groping upwards." It is an application of at least two perceptions. The first is a denial of the *de gustibus* maxim and an assertion that some values are better than other values. A taste for string quartets is better than a taste for champagnes; it is better to enjoy poetry than pornography; it is better to want to commune with unspoiled nature than to like Sunday driving on parkways. What basis can there possibly be for such evaluations of values? I believe that in all these instances, and others, the values must be rated according to the degree to which they are "consciousness expanding": the higher values in the scale are those that stretch distinctively human (as against animal) faculties and potentialities the most. It may have been Socrates who first argued for this fundamental basis of valuation, but just what the basis may be is irrelevant at the moment. The basic insight on which Tribe draws is that there are criteria, albeit difficult to express, for evaluating values themselves. Then, in accordance with Mill's criterion, one consideration in reaching environmental decisions is the degree to which the decisions reached and the process of reaching them strengthen adherence to higher values relative to lower ones.

A second basic perception in groping upwards is that at any given time, the scale of values can only be vaguely perceived. In the preceding paragraph, to make things concrete, I conjectured what the underlying scale might be. But that was only a conjecture, and even if in some sense "correct", it was inherently vague. To stick with that scale for one more sentence, we cannot measure "consciousness expandingness," and we can learn how experiences rate on that scale only by experiencing them.

More than esthetics is involved. To revert to Mill, one of the values involved is the duty of a society to inculcate higher values rather than lower ones in its members, to nudge them upwards along the scale. But which direction is up is not clearly perceived and never will be. It is very easy to feel confident that a taste for nature is superior to contentment with crowded beaches; it is not so easy to rate a taste for nature against a concern for providing respectable employment opportunities for blacks—and that is the kind of perplexity that frequently arises.

Laurence Tribe points out that our values at any time are largely what past decisions and experiences have made them, and that one of the consequences of our current choices is to mold our future values. We must recognize that our current scale of values is only tentative, but it is the only scale we have. We must use it as best we can to make choices that will strengthen our adherence to higher values and to make our value system more like what it "ought" to be. I take it that our values "ought" to be those that stand the test of time, and that do not lead to choices that we shall soon regret, as we now regret the annihilation of the buffalo and the destruction of the forests of the Michigan peninsula. But in any event I agree with Tribe that the processes by which we make our choices that shape our values ought *themselves* to be ones that reflect the best sense we can achieve, at any particular time, of the sorts of values we are coming to hold.

It seems to me that the major practical import of groping upwards is that we should appraise each option, including each option for appraising options and for structuring choices among them, in terms of the extent to which it promotes or interferes with each of the "higher values" that it seems likely to affect. Respect for nature, for example, now seems such a value, and any option that expresses and exemplifies respect for nature is to that extent preferable to one that does not.

The Tocks Island controversy illustrates both the potentialities of this approach and the perplexities it raises. Consider the potentialities first. One of the benefits for which the Tocks Island Dam was designed was to assure a low flow of 3,000 cubic feet per second at Trenton. This flow is desirable for a number of reasons, high among them that it would keep the saline waters of the Delaware Estuary safely below the Torresdale intake of the Philadelphia water supply system. The facts are somewhat in dispute, but let us accept them in order to examine the principle at work. Let us suppose also that the recreational potential of the upper Delaware is at least as well served without the dam as with it, nature loving being a higher value than picknicking and water skiing (even according to most picknickers and water skiers). But, since the recreation benefits preponderate in the benefit-cost evaluation of the dam, if we reduce them to zero or less in this way, the benefit-cost ratio will become unfavorable and the dam will not qualify for construction. Would this be a disaster for Philadelphia? In fact not. There are other ways to protect its water intake, some not environmentally destructive at all.

Now, the Philadelphia water supply and the costs of other ways of protecting it in drought years are very practical considerations, but they cannot claim to serve higher values. On the basis of Tribe's analysis they should play a subordinate role in making the decision, and should by no means be determinative. We should learn to sacrifice practical considerations in favor of higher values, and each time we do so we shall strengthen our ability to do so in the future. Then future generations will not look back on us with contempt for having desecrated the Tocks Island reach of the river to save a few tens of millions of dollars in assuring Philadelphia's water supply.

In short, to inject humane values into environmental decisions we must undertake a serious commitment to them, and give them pride of place over practical considerations. In fact, however, the priorities are just the reverse in current practice. The 3,000 cfs at Trenton has come to be regarded as what Robert Socolow calls a "golden number"—an absolute requirement that has to be met by any plan of development, without regard to its merits in other respects. In that particular application, groping upwards speaks unequivocally. It is wrong to design the development of the Tocks Island region subject to the requirement that 3,000 cfs be provided at Trenton at all times; it is right to infringe this practical requirement if significant "higher values" can be attained by so doing.

But there are other aspects of the decision that are not so cleanly disposed of by taking higher values into account. The main controversy, indeed, concerns the amount and nature of the recreational opportunities to be provided. The situation can be sketched as follows: the Tocks Island Dam would create a large lake—37 miles long—in what is now an only slightly spoiled rural countryside stretching along the Delaware River from the Delaware Water Gap to Port Jervis. Exurbanization is already encroaching, but has not yet destroyed the basically nineteenth century farm country character of the area. The Tocks Island Reservoir and Delaware Water Gap National Recreation Area would change all that. There would be a majestic dam rising to 160 feet above the current stream bed, beaches to accommodate 59,000 people, parking lots and access freeways for 33,000 cars. The plan has varied from time to time, but in one version the park was planned for a capacity of 150,000 in its 47,000 acres. One doesn't need much imagination to hear the cacophony of the transistor radios.

Now, do respect for humane values and concern for good qualities in the governed point in the direction of building a dam, or do they indicate, rather, that we should endeavor to preserve this fragment of our heritage? This could be done, as has been proposed, by establishing the park (to arrest exurbanization) without constructing the reservoir or the mass-recreation facilities. A large body of opinion, indeed, sees the path of virtue leading in that direction.

But now let us contemplate the map. The proposed reservoir and park lie in a unique position within easy driving distance of the first and fourth largest standard metropolitan statistical areas in the country. The poor and near poor of New York, Newark, and Philadelphia have little use for open countryside and second-growth wilderness. They canoe not, neither do they hunt. But many of them would appreciate a family outing on a sweltering Sunday to a well-equipped picnic grove or a fresh-water beach. The proposed park provides an ideal, large-scale locale for such facilities. Would the "sum" of good qualities in the governed thereby be increased, along with their Sunday enjoyment? There would be nature walks, rental canoes, even a 900-acre wildlife preserve. Very likely some of the visitors would have their interest in canoeing and hunting ignited by this close exposure. And of course, the family picnic is itself an American tradition with some claim to preservation.[a]

In this application it is by no means clear which decision maximizes the sum of good qualities in the governed, or better affirms our dedication to humane values, even when disagreements about which values are more "humane" are temporarily assumed away. Untrammelled wilderness and unspoiled cultural artifacts are higher values, but so also is inexpensive outdoor recreation for city dwellers. The appeal to humane values, in this instance and in many others, is obviously not decisive.

Yet, even here, Tribe's appeal is not futile. It reminds us that a conventional benefit-cost or cost effectiveness analysis wrongly neglects such considerations completely. The conventional method of quantification attempts to measure recreation benefits by means

---

[a]I must mention that any implied support of the Tocks Island project is intended merely to force an issue of principle. In fact there are such technical difficulties in the design of the project that it seems unlikely to work out as idyllically as described in the text.

of the number of visitor-days appraised at rather flaccid values—in the Tocks Island case ranging from $.65 a day for sightseeing to $2.50 per day for hunting—based on market or cost considerations and purposely avoiding any attempt to evaluate the quality of the experience or its contribution to increasing the sum of good qualities in the visitor. Nowhere does conventional analysis admit any purpose higher than ephemeral enjoyment. Since there are such purposes, and since everyone knows that there are, groping upwards demands only common honesty when it insists that higher values be taken into account.

If we knew which values should be deemed higher and which lower, a commitment to respect for higher values would go a long way toward settling the problems of environmental decision making; but in many instances we do not know, or cannot agree on, what the hierarchy of values is. As things stand, we have to contend with many perplexities that no one can resolve definitively: we shall know whether we have decided wisely only after we and our children have lived with the results, if then. But at least we shall not decide shamefully if every decision is designed to promote humane values as they are understood, however dimly, at the time it is taken. Tribe urges us to wrestle openly with the humane values involved whenever an environmental decision is to be taken.

SOME ASPECTS OF IMPLEMENTATION

We have now argued a hard doctrine. In making decision about environmental matters, cognizance, and even priority, has to be given to "humane values," "higher values," and so on. In so arguing, we do not imply that this is not already done. In fact, it is sometimes done; humane values are too insistent to be denied (remember the quotation from Arthur Maass, p. 156). This is just where the stress and dissatisfaction comes from. Nevertheless, we frequently do not admit that we are motivated by higher values.[b] They are considered to be inappropriate in hard-headed analysis, and indeed, the analyst is constantly enjoined to keep his personal preferences (i.e., higher values) out of his analysis. Our argument entails that higher values do have a proper and necessary place in any analysis. We now consider how this place can be provided without sneaking them in surreptitiously.

For higher values to be injected into a policy analysis there must be widespread agreement about them—or at least about the qualities

[b]This is one of Robert Socolow's "failures of discourse" (see his essay in this volume).

to be sought in the processes for arriving at such substantive value agreement. Fortunately, in any society there is often such agreement, though this circumstance is frequently denied. The denial arises from confusing what is "objectively provable" with what is generally agreed. The fact that there is no way to "prove" that denuding forests is bad is perfectly consistent with universal agreement that it *is* bad. Broad agreement on what is good and what is bad, however, is not sufficient to establish a coherent scale of values. The separate values often conflict, as we have seen in the Tocks Island case, and there is often no clear ranking of the priorities among them.

One method for establishing priorities among conflicting values has been proposed by John Hammond.[4] Although I feel that we have to amend Hammond's proposal substantially, it is worth considering here. Hammond's notion is to construct a rating scale in which the relative importances of the different values at stake are rated on a scale of 1 to 10, or perhaps merely ranked. Then one is to score each of the alternatives with respect to each of the values with a system of marks such as "+" "0", and "—". Finally, one ranks the alternatives, giving the highest ranks to the alternatives for which the highest scores tend to be associated with the highest-ranking values.

There is a fundamental difficulty with applying this sort of proposal to social decisions, environmental or otherwise. The relative importance of the values at stake in any particular decision is not an absolute, once-for-all matter. Among other things, it depends a good deal on how well those values are being served by prior or contemporary decisions. To construct such a rating scale we have to answer a question like, "Which is more important, preservation of salt marshes or provision of respectable jobs for blacks?" And such a question is inherently unanswerable. The only respectable response to it is another question: "How many acres of salt marsh and how many blacks without respectable jobs do we now have?"

We have seen in the case of Tocks Island that it was both irrelevant and impossible to assign relative priorities to the value of recreation for a comparatively small number in a comparatively natural setting as against recreation for a large number using highly developed facilities. We could formulate the Tocks Island question sensibly only by recognizing that the facilities there would be net additions to the supplies of recreation opportunities of both types available to the same population of users. We don't really have to be able to decide which type of use is of higher value "absolutely," but only which type is more urgently needed in view of the alternatives to Tocks. Judgments may still differ, and will, but the problem is vastly more manageable.

With this amendment, the ranking suggestion appears helpful. The bread-and-butter consequences of alternatives can be compared by a standard benefit-cost analysis. The higher value consequences can be campared, nonquantitatively, by a table in which the different higher values affected are listed in order of their urgency in the applicable context, and each alternative is given a nonquantitative score for each of the higher values as well as a quantitative score for the benefits and costs that can be assigned reasonably firm monetary values. Persons of good will scrutinizing such a table can still disagree, but they will be taking all values into account and improving their capacity to do so in future instances. That is about as far as groping upwards can take us on any single decision. For the rest, the process depends on facing choices among values candidly and accumulating experience.

So much for the staff work performed by the policy analyst. Staff work is not likely to be effective, however, unless it takes account of the rest of the decision process in which it is immersed, and in particular of the decision maker whom it is intended to serve. Who is the "Decision Maker"? Several of the participants addressed themselves to this question, and were unanimous in finding that he is plural. In the Tocks Island case, the decision makers appear to be the governors of the affected states plus the United States Congress. In general, even when the organization chart shows a single locus of decision, the facts of the case indicate that the nominal decision maker is not unfettered but must seek a reconciliation among the decisions advocated by other more-or-less influential and more-or-less numerous individuals. The so-called Decision Maker is in fact a process of reconciling the desires, claims, and powers of a variety of contending groups.

The circumstance that makes this process manageable is that all the contenders at any time avow allegiance to roughly the same basic set of higher values. The saying is that "disagreements concern means rather than ends." The assertion is often debatable, but belief in it makes conflict manageable. Public policy decisions are therefore argued out by people who, for various reasons, give primacy to different considerations. It is becoming fashionable to perceive the virtues of this circumstance—in effect, to advocate advocacy. My own feeling is that extolling advocacy in public affairs is a bit like lauding the virtues of gravity or friction.[c]

[c]Now that the issue has come up, candor compels me to disclose that I personally am rather in favor of the law of gravitation (in spite of its occasional tragic consequences), but am bitterly opposed to the second law of thermodynamics. And I believe that anyone's attitude toward advocacy in public affairs is about equally consequential.

Still, at least one comment is in order. The instances always cited for the efficacy of advocacy are legal disputes and scientific controversy. It is not pointed out nearly so habitually that those are also the two areas in which, over the course of time, very strict canons have developed for the admissibility of evidence and the validity of reasoning. Severe discipline severely enforced is what distinguishes the two exemplary types of adversary proceedings. Just contrast the logical rigor that you would expect to find in a paper called "On the Effects of Ions of NaF on Dental Enamel" with what you would encounter at a public forum on fluoridating the town's water supply. How differently even the same man would speak in those two contexts!

The familiar examples, then, confirm the efficacy of highly disciplined advocacy, but have little to say about the much less constrained version that is employed in public decision making. I know of no more vivid exposition of the shortcomings of the political version of advocacy than Robert Socolow's "Failures of Discourse" in this volume. He has caught and summarized nearly all the pathologies of public undisciplined argumentation too well for me to recapitulate.

The significant issue, then, about advocacy is how to constrain it. The pertinence of the classic examples of fruitful controversy is the lesson that advocacy can be constrained even when passion-engendering issues are at stake, as they are in both law and science. They also show that the social arrangements for controlling advocacy are likely to be very different in different circumstances.

The participants in our project were well aware of the tendency of uncontrolled advocacy to misfire, and were accordingly unwilling to expose decisions about environmental policies to its perils. There were therefore several proposals for the establishment of a relatively neutral institute or institution, endowed with great prestige and scientific expertise, to sort out the claims and arguments of the advocates and produce an authoritative appraisal and recommendation. The pronouncement of this neutral scientific review institute would not be entirely binding on the Decision Maker but would incorporate the best overall evaluation that skilled and disinterested scientific judgment could produce. It was also recognized that such a "neutral" evaluative group, no matter how prestigious, would inevitably enter the decision making process as an advocate for its own conclusions.

I have to cast doubt on the feasibility of creating an institute of respected nonpartisan partisans. It has already been tried, to a degree, and the results are just what might be expected. The National

Academy of Sciences is being appealed to more and more frequently to perform this function in public debates that have scientific aspects, including, in fact, debates about environmental policy. The conclusions of the National Academy have not been accepted, on the whole, as demonstrably neutral and authoritative. The prejudices and preconceptions of the scientists do show, confirming Private Willis's deep thought that

> Every boy and every gal
>   That's born into this world alive
> Is either a little liberal
>   Or else a little conservative,
> Tra-la-la

Scientists, like everyone else, are subject to the influence of their personal status and preferences.

Both law and science, in their different ways, recognize that there are no neutrals and limit their disciplining of argumentation to imposing constraints on the behavior of the adversaries. Something analogous is required in public discussions of public problems, but it will evolve, if it does, gradually, and I am not in a position to suggest it. Here, too, we must grope upwards, on a procedural level.

I do, however, have one positive suggestion to make: that in the environmental field we arrange matters so that no one party receives the great preponderance of the ammunition.[d] At present there are no such arrangements and, as an example, in the case of Tocks Island only the Corps of Engineers had the wherewithal to conduct a genuine study and analysis of the situation. Here, and typically, the dice were loaded in favor of the big battalions. This is a situation that can be corrected more easily than is often supposed. One method would be as follows. At the stage where a feasibility study is seen to be in order, the funds appropriated for that purpose could be turned over to a Court of Environmental Affairs rather than to one of the interested parties. The court could then invite interested organizations, agencies, and people to submit evidence of legitimate concern, somewhat analogous to the current procedures for being granted standing to intervene in a legal proceeding. After the admissions have been granted, the court would divide among the admitted parties both the budget and the tasks. The results of the analyses would be

---

[d]This is really a special case of Laurence Tribe's insistence that the processes from which we start in environmental matters should assiduously avoid preassigned domination in any form.

argued out, as at present, before the public and the cognizant public officials and bodies.

The sole change from present practice at that stage would be that no evidence which is only unilaterally available would be admissible at any official proceeding. "New facts and findings" could be introduced only with the permission of the court, which would assure that before they were introduced all parties of standing had fair opportunity to inspect and audit them. Such a change in procedure would not entail duplication of effort. Presumably the Corps of Engineers would still be assigned the tasks of performing the test borings and making the hydrologic studies for a project such as Tocks. But the other interested parties would have the opportunity and facilities to audit the Corps' work thoroughly and to make their own analyses of the data developed by the Corps.

This proposal appeals to me as a first step toward lifting the level of semipublic debate in the environmental field in a way that is cognizant of Laurence Tribe's reminder that devotion to process is the beginning of environmental wisdom—the only way to avoid some of the failures of discourse that Robert Socolow has catalogued. Some of Socolow's "failures," of course, arise from the central problem of this project: the admission that higher values are legitimate considerations in environmental decisions. Those failures will be cured when we accept the commitment to public purpose, to maximizing the sum of good qualities, to the advancement of higher values.

This essay is further evidence of my assertion that there are no neutrals. I was assigned the task of reporting on the work of others. But I see that I have not done that. I have come to my own conclusions and have advocated them. Let me close then by conceding that I am groping too, and that my conclusions are no more authoritative than those of the authors on whom I have passed judgment.

It would have been more comfortable if we could have emerged from this long effort with a formula for measuring a project's contribution to humane values and a handbook for applying the formula. Instead we have arrived at the conclusion that no such formula or handbook is possible, now or ever. Environmental decisions were seen to be part of the human experience in which wisdom is acquired by earnest seeking rather than by the application of pat formulas, and in which each decision's contribution to wisdom (or detraction therefrom) may be as significant as its overt results. In the environmental field, the road to wisdom is a decision process that forces explicit recognition that the environment has values that transcend the economic calculus.

NOTES

1. Arthur Maass, "Benefit-Cost Analysis: Its Relevance to Public Investment Decisions," *Quarterly Journal of Economics* LXXX (May 1966): 208–209, 211–212.

2. The point is developed by Laurence Tribe in "Policy Science: Analysis or Ideology?" *Philosophy and Public Affairs* 2 (Fall 1972):68–72, 85–89, 105–106.

3. J. S. Mill, "Representative Government," in *On Liberty, Representative Government, The Subjection of Women, Three Essays by John Stuart Mill*, ed. Millicent G. Fawcett (London: Oxford University, 1969), Chap. II, p. 168.

4. Hammond, John S. III, "Bringing Order in the Selection of a College," *Personnel and Guidance Journal* 43 (March 1965):654–660.

Index

About the Contributors

Harvey Brooks is Benjamin Peirce Professor of Technology and Public Policy, Harvard University.

Robert Dorfman is David A. Wells Professor of Political Economy, Harvard University.

Charles Frankel is Old Dominion Professor of Philosophy and Public Affairs, Columbia University.

Henry S. Rowen is Professor of Public Management, Graduate School of Business, Stanford University.

Corinne S. Schelling is Assistant Executive Officer, American Academy of Arts and Sciences.

Robert Socolow is Associate Professor of Aerospace and Mechanical Studies, and a member of the Center for Environmental Studies, Princeton University.

Irene Taviss Thomson is Assistant Professor of Sociology, Fairleigh Dickinson University.

Laurence H. Tribe is Professor of Law, Harvard University

John Voss is Executive Officer, American Academy of Arts and Sciences.